DEFENDER OF THE FAITH

DEFENDER
OF THE FAITH
The High Court of Mississippi
1817-1875

MEREDITH LANG

UNIVERSITY PRESS OF MISSISSIPPI
JACKSON
1977

Library of Congress Cataloging in Publication Data

Lang, Meredith.
    Defender of the faith.

    Bibliography: p.
    Includes index.
    1. Mississippi. High Court of Errors and Appeals—
History.   I. Title.
KFM7112.L36   347′.762′03309   77-7971
ISBN 0-87805-033-7

CONTENTS

To the contemporary ear the sounds of the high court of Mississippi in its antebellum period have a strangely anachronistic quality. Yet, the opinions contained in volumes one through thirty-nine of the Mississippi Reports have much to teach about the role of a state appellate court functioning as both the exponent of specific public policies and, on a grander scale, as the defender of the basic values held by a society. What is more, that defense was aggressive and militant, whether the high court was thinking on the plane of a noble idealism, which informed its opinions in the area of criminal justice, or on the level of a savage fanaticism, which pervaded the cases in the law of manumission. In fact, these two chapters of the following study—manumission and criminal justice—illustrate the tension in Mississippi, epitomized so vividly on the court, between the opposing forces of parochial and national creeds.

The parochial faith took time to crystallize—the process required almost a generation. As it hardened to the mold attained in the 1850s, the high court reflected this subtle transformation between 1817 and 1860 from the open to the closed society. Another change in the mood of the court—this one abrupt and dramatic—took place in 1869 with the coming of congressional reconstruction. But although the court then, too, accurately mirrored the political ambiance, that change was too artificial, too quick to be deeply felt. It was, in short, superimposed by an alien power.

Internal doctrinal disputes did crop up on the high court periodically before the Civil War. There was the grave schism over the issue of the rights in Mississippi of slaves emancipated elsewhere, as well as the division over the enforceability of a contract made in violation of a provision in the constitution of 1832 prohibiting the introduction of slaves as merchandise. But these rifts were either harmonized before the war, or the dispute was of a technical nature. To a man, the justices were devoted to the three articles of faith on which Mississippi society rested: slavery, state sovereignty, and the compact theory of government. Even if the justices were not all secessionists in the precise meaning of that term, as a court they spoke with one mind on the critical issues confronting it.

Only in the area of reconstruction theory did the Mississippi High Court suffer a loss of confidence, even of identity. But in 1865 it was an entirely different world. The institution on which the faith had rested was destroyed, and the relevance of the old faith to the new world was not yet clearly perceived. Chapter 6 traces this pilgrimage of the court through purgatory—a sad finale to the story of a still proud, once defiant high court.

DEFENDER OF THE FAITH

CHAPTER I

Of the Nature of Government

The purpose of this chapter is twofold. First, on a descriptive-narrative plane, the chapter examines virtually all the cases of a public or quasi-public character decided by the Mississippi High Court from 1817 to 1861 [1] which posed questions of state or federal constitutional law. At this level obvious parallelisms with such national themes as judicial review, due process, and the great ends of all constitutional governments as articulated by the United States Supreme Court are emphasized. The discussion is topical, not chronological. Second, on a more analytical level, the chapter examines those few pre-Civil War cases which seemed to contain, either in their rationale or dicta, the essential elements of a particular philosophy of government which led ultimately, in the political sector, to secession.

Circumstantial evidence supports a theory that the Mississippi High Court was the judicial counterpart of the states' rights school of American political thought represented by John C.

---

[1] Although many of the cases dealing with problems of reconstruction are also of a public or governmental nature, they are omitted entirely from this chapter because a separate chapter is devoted exclusively to this subject (see Chapter 6). Cases arising under the contract clause of the federal Constitution are also omitted. See Chapter 2 for a treatment of this topic.

Calhoun, Jefferson Davis, and John A. Quitman. This is not to say that the Mississippi justices were all secessionists, any more than the Mississippi politicians of this period were all secessionists.[2] In fact, William S. Sharkey, a Whig and chief justice of the high court from 1832 to 1850, remained a "Unionist" to the final hour. The thesis of the second phase of the chapter, rather, is simply that the Mississippi High Court knowingly endorsed a constitutional philosophy which became the formula for the right of secession, even though the court was a mere bystander to the act itself.

One reason why the Mississippi political-constitutional thought of the antebellum era holds a fascination for the contemporary reader lies in a basic ambiguity existing in its constitutional polity between national beliefs and the parochial faith. The high court in particular could clasp totally such concepts as judicial review and due process, and at the same time it could ignore totally the national theory of the government formed in 1787—a government of the people, by the people, and for the people. Furthermore, even though its contacts with the doctrine of state sovereignty were oblique, the court eventually became more sensitive to the tensions created by that doctrine than any of the other branches of the state government. The rationale of a particular group of cases decided in this period—those dealing with emancipation and manumission—rested exclusively on the state sovereignty issue, and the degree of justice meted out in those cases depended to an appreciable degree on its validity.

Let us now survey the case literature of the period on the first level of descriptive narrative. The issues in these early cases concern concrete demonstrations of legislative power, while the

---

[2] Jefferson Davis, although believing steadfastly in the "abstract right" of secession as a constitutional prerogative, never believed that the time had come to exercise the right, although as a loyal Mississippian he, of course, acquiesced in the decision of January 9, 1861, to secede. His own position on this matter remained virtually poised on the brink throughout the 1850s.

holdings establish the extent to which that power may be exercised. The rationale examines such concepts as judicial review, due process, the separation of powers, and the nature of American federalism; while the dicta deal with the themes of popular sovereignty, the social compact, and the aims of constitutional government.

As for the specific exercises of legislative power, *Runnels* v. *State* [3] early established that the legislature could not constitutionally abolish the office of clerk of the probate court on the ground that the office had been created under the constitution of 1817 (art. 5, § 11). From *Williams* v. *Cammack* [4] came the rule that the legislature could provide different rates of tax for the improvement of levees on lands according to their distances from the Mississippi River. The general power of taxation being within the scope of the legislative grant, a particular exercise of it could not be invalidated by the judiciary because that tribunal believed the particular exercise was contrary to wise policy or the principles of natural justice. In the same case it was also decided the tax in question did not violate the constitutional principle that "all free men are equal in rights" (art. 1, § 1), since that principle referred to equality in political rights and had no reference to legislative acts regulating the domestic policy and business affairs of the people. On the other hand a statute giving to a surety the right of moving for a judgment against his principal for money paid by him as security was held in *Smith's Administrator* v. *Smith* [5] to violate the same constitutional prohibition against conferring exclusive privileges, because it favored a particular class of creditors over all others.

In *Brown* v. *Beatty* [6] the court upheld the power of eminent domain as to the taking of private property for the construction of railroads as an inherent element of sovereignty, over the ob-

[3] 1 Miss. (Walk.) 146 (1823).   [4] 27 Miss. 209, 218 (1854).
[5] 2 Miss. (1 How.) 102 (1834).   [6] 34 Miss. 227, 240 (1857).

jection that railroad corporations are private rather than public in nature. It was the view of the court that the construction of railroads and other internal improvements were in keeping with the right and duty of the state to promote the welfare and happiness of its members, to facilitate and cheapen transportation, and to increase commerce among its citizens.

Yet the power of eminent domain, according to *Thompson* v. *Grand Gulf R.R.*,[7] should be exercised "only in the strictest justice toward the owner of the property." Accordingly, the compensation must *precede* the taking, and a mere judgment for the amount of damages assessed was not deemed compensation. *Isom* v. *Mississippi Central R.R.*[8] determined that it was beyond the power of the legislature to direct the trial court in a condemnation proceeding to fix the damages sustained by the owner to allow, in extinguishment of the claim for damages, the benefits which would result to the owner from the construction of the road through his land. The judges ruled that the ascertainment of damages sustained on account of the appropriation of private property to a public use was a judicial, not a legislative act.

A deviation from the constitution by the legislature in the mode prescribed of proposing constitutional amendments to the people was upheld in *Green* v. *Weller*.[9] The court permitted a quorum of the members of each house to pass proposed constitutional amendments instead of insisting upon a two-thirds majority, as provided by the constitution of 1832.

A leading case of 1860—*Alcorn* v. *Hamer* [10]—found no infirmity in a revenue measure of the legislature which provided that a tax enacted for the purpose of repairing the levee of the Mississippi River in designated counties should not be collected if a majority of the voters defeated the tax in an election to be conducted for that purpose. Plaintiffs (taxpayers in the affected

[7] 4 Miss. (3 How.) 240 (1839).   [8] 36 Miss. 300 (1858).   [9] 32 Miss. 650 (1856).
[10] 38 Miss. 652 (1860).

counties) argued that the legislature, as the sole repository of legislative power, had no right to relinquish it to the whole people of the state and thus change the distribution of power ordained by the constitution. The high court distinguished between acts requiring their adoption by the people as a condition precedent to their validity (which are unconstitutional), and those acts taking effect immediately upon their legislative enactment, but subject to defeat by a condition subsequent (which are constitutional).

Due process was a cherished concept in the pre-Civil War epoch of the high court. In 1850, the state legislature had vested title to lands delinquent for nonpayment of taxes in the state of Mississippi, without notice or hearing to the parties affected. In a lengthy opinion the court held in *Griffin* v. *Mixon* [11] that such a gross abuse of legislative power violated due process and was therefore void. Addressing itself generally to the spirit of due process, the court quoted Mr. Justice Story's dictum in *Wilkinson* v. *Leland* [12] that "the fundamental maxims of a free government . . . require, that the rights of personal liberty and private property should be held sacred"; and that "the power to violate and disregard them" is "repugnant to the common principles of justice and civil liberty." [13] Furthermore, the court went on to register its indignation over this example of legislative excess because the Mississippi constitution specifically contained a "due course of law" clause [14] forbidding such an arbitrary exercise of illegitimate power:

If upon *general principles,* the power of the legislature is thus restricted, how much more important is it under the guarded provisions of *our Constitution,* that we should scrutinize the act in question by which the land of this defendant, without notice,—actual or constructive,—without his consent, without compensation, without necessity

---

[11] 38 Miss. 424 (1860).   [12] 27 U.S. (2 Pet.) 627, 657 (1829).
[13] 38 Miss. at 436.   [14] Miss. Const. art. I, § 10 (1832).

for public use, and without "due course of law", is attempted to be wrested from him, and, for a nominal consideration, vested by the power of legislation alone in this plaintiff. It is not to be *presumed*, that such a power exists, in this State, at this day, under our Constitution.[15]

Similarly, a city ordinance by which the marshall was directed to seize and sell all hogs found running at large within the city of Vicksburg was held unconstitutional in *Donovan* v. *Mayor and Council of Vicksburg,* [16] because the ordinance failed to provide notice or trial and an opportunity to protect one's rights to property before being deprived of it. The court reasoned as follows:

Upon such notice, and with an opportunity allowed him to show cause against the enforcement of the ordinance in the particular case, he might have been able to show that the hogs had just broken his inclosure, when they were seized, and that he had not time to retake and secure them, or that the inclosure had been torn down for the necessary purposes during the raging of fire in the city or by a tornado, and that it was impossible under the circumstances to confine them again before they were seized; or he might have even been able to show that they were turned loose by the procurement of the parties having them seized and sold.[17]

Almost simultaneously the United States Supreme Court was noting in *Scott* v. *Sandford* [18] its dissatisfaction with an act of Congress which attempted to prohibit the citizens of the slave states from taking their slave property into the territories [19] on the ground that this, too, constituted a denial of due process. Tucked away in that celebrated opinion is the following language:

[15] 38 Miss. at 436.   [16] 29 Miss. 247 (1855).   [17] *Ibid.*, 249.

[18] 60 U.S. (19 How.) 393 (1857). The Court held that the word "citizen" in the United States Constitution does not embrace a member of the Negro race and accordingly that Dred Scott, a Negro, could not bring suit in a United States district court in Missouri on the basis of diversity of citizenship to establish his right to freedom.

[19] Act of March 6, 1820, ch. 22, 5 Stat. 545 (The Missouri Compromise). This attempt to resolve the slavery issue provided that Missouri should be admitted as a slave state but prohibited slavery in the remaining parts of the Louisiana Territory above 36° 30′ (the southern boundary of Missouri). The act was held unconstitutional in the Dred Scott case.

Thus the rights of property are united with the rights of person, and placed on the same ground by the fifth amendment to the Constitution, which provides that no person shall be deprived of life, liberty, and property without due process of law. . . . And if the Constitution recognizes the right of property of the master in a slave, and makes no distinction between that property and other property owned by a citizen, no tribunal, acting under the authority of the United States, whether it be legislative, executive, or judicial, has a right to draw such a distinction, or deny to it the benefit of the provisions and guarantees which have been provided for the protection of private property against the encroachments of the Government.[20]

As one turns to the subject of judicial review, the cases take on a broader significance. From *Runnels* v. *State* comes the first instance in which the high court held an act of the legislature unconstitutional, a task which the court approached with "caution and circumspection" in view of the "delicacy of the situation" and the "magnitude of the case." [21] Regrettably, however, no argument comparable to that of Marshall's in *Marbury* v. *Madison* [22] was constructed to support the imperative of judicial scrutiny of legislative acts. The court reached that result by tying two propositions together: one, that the Mississippi constitution requires a separation of powers into three distinct departments; and two, that no department may exercise any power belonging to either of the others. Immediately follows the conclusion: "Upon this court, then, devolves the high and important duty, of rescuing from legislative violation, those contracts, which have their origin in the constitution, and are placed beyond the reach of legislative control and interference." [23] Precisely why it is the duty of the court, rather than the duty of each department, to keep within its constitutional bounds, was the question not faced by the court, and in effect, its legal conclusion only

[20] Scott v. Sandford, 60 U.S. (19 How.) 393, 450–51 (1856).
[21] 1 Miss. (Walk.) 146 (1823).   [22] 5 U.S. (1 Cranch) 137 (1803).
[23] Runnels v. State, 1 Miss. (Walk.) 146, 147 (1823).

begged that question. A later Mississippi case found the duty in the proposition that the "judiciary . . . are bound by the constitution, and sworn to support it," [24] which was, incidentally, the last argument made by Marshall in *Marbury* v. *Madison*.

In time, most Mississippi courts either took the power of judicial review for granted, or suggested that since there had to be some curb put on legislative abuses of its power, the judiciary was the natural, logical department to impose it. [25]

So far, at least, the values of the Mississippi High Court and those of the Supreme Court of the United States were strikingly congruent. This harmony was further emphasized when the Mississippi court loftily announced in dicta in *Dennistoun and Co.* v. *Potts* [26] that the purpose of government is to protect individual rights. Incidentally, the holding in that case was only that a justice of the peace in Adams County could take, under a statute of 1836, the acknowledgment of a mortgage conveying land and slaves in Washington County where the land was legally recorded. And when the high court said in *Thompson* v. *Grand Gulf R.R.* that "life, liberty and property are three great objects of governmental protection," [27] it was only repeating what Justice Johnson once said in his concurring opinions in *Gibbons* v. *Ogden:* [28] "The great and paramount purpose was to unite this mass of wealth and power for the protection of the humblest individual; his rights, civil and political, his interests and prosperity, are the sole *end;* the rest are nothing but the *means.*" [29]

As one moves away from the concepts of judicial review, due process, and the great ends of government into the more metaphysical realms of sovereignty, the social compact theory, and

[24] Green v. Weller, 32 Miss. 650, 705 (1856).
[25] Griffin v. Mixon, 38 Miss. 424, 448–50 (1860).   [26] 26 Miss. 2, 31 (1853).
[27] 4 Miss. (3 How.) 240, 248 (1839).   [28] 22 U.S. (9 Wheat.) 1 (1824).
[29] *Ibid.*, 223. The Court held that acts of the state of New York, which granted to Robert Fulton and Robert Livingston the exclusive right to navigate all the waters within that state with boats moved by fire or steam, violated the interstate commerce clause of the Constitution.

the implication of certain inalienable rights, the sounds of the Mississippi High Court and the United States Supreme Court become highly dissonant. That sovereignty resides in the people was never denied in Mississippi jurisprudence. On the contrary, it crept into the early opinions as a fundamental premise from which one could embark on almost any major argument in constitutional law. But in Mississippi the idea of popular sovereignty took on a particular connotation. Passages from three major opinions of the Mississippi High Court written between 1817 and 1861, all of which contained a reference to the word "sovereignty" in either dicta or rationale, appear below. Each passage will be analyzed in turn in respect to its particular usage of the word.

The first quotation is from one of the earliest cases to be argued before the Mississippi High Court—*Harry* v. *Decker* [30]—decided in 1818. It was an interesting case on the facts. Taking with him his three slaves, one John Decker moved from Virginia to Indiana in the year 1784, three years before the Ordinance of 1787 prohibited slavery in the Northwest Territory. He remained there until, in 1816, Indiana became a state with a clause in its constitution prohibiting slavery. He then brought the Negroes to Mississippi and sold them, whereupon they petitioned for their freedom in the chancery court of Mississippi. Decker defended on the ground, first, that the Ordinance of 1787 and the Indiana Constitution, if applied to this case, would violate the treaty of cession from Virginia to the United States, as well as the Constitution of the United States; and second, that the provision against slavery, both in the ordinance and Indiana Constitution was prospective and did not apply to existing slaves, since that would violate vested rights. The court held, however, for the petitioners in an extraordinary opinion containing the following allusion to popular sovereignty:

[30] 1 Miss. (Walk.) 36 (1818).

In all governments whatsoever there must be of necessity, and in the nature of things, a supreme irresistible absolute and uncontroled authority, in which the "jura summi imperii," or the rights of sovereignty reside, and when we speak of sovereignty in this sense, it is in contradistinction of the powers given under a constitution, or the powers of a limited government, that a constitution emanates from and is a part of that sovereignty in its most extensive sense, as residing in the people, is universally acknowledged by all those best acquainted with the theory and principles of our government, that the same power that creates, can change, alter or destroy, is a consequence too clear to require it to be supported by proof.[31]

That passage was written by an anonymous justice in 1818, almost a quarter of a century before the slavery issue was to grip the state. Sovereignty in the context of that opinion is expressly distinguished from "government." Nowhere is there any suggestion of an identity between the "people" in whom sovereignty resides and the state in its corporate capacity. Thirty-eight years later, the dissenting opinion in *Green* v. *Weller* made such a suggestion:

The people in their aggregate or sovereign capacity in distinct and express terms, have prescribed the manner in which the [state] Constitution may be altered or amended.

In laying down this proposition, I am, however, not to be understood as meaning that the *State, or the people constituting the State, have not at all times and under all circumstances, in the plenitude of their sovereignty,* the right to alter or abolish, at will, the existing Constitution and government, and to ordain, in their stead, another Constitution or form of government better calculated to promote their interests. . . . (Emphasis added.) [32]

It is immaterial that this passage appears as dicta in the dissent, not the majority opinion. In fact, a stronger case can be made for the argument that popular sovereignty, as used by the court in the majority opinion, was equivalent to the state *legislature.* The issue in the case was whether a constitutional amend-

[31] *Ibid.*, 40.   [32] 32 Miss. 650, 693 (1856).

ment of 1856 was valid, since the state legislature had not proposed it in the exact manner prescribed by the constitution of 1832. The majority held that it was a valid amendment nonetheless, on the ground that the relevant constitutional clause should receive such a construction as not to trammel the exercise of the right of amendment, and on the further ground that an act of the legislature valid on its face may not be looked into by the judiciary for irregularities in the manner by which it became law. The implication of the majority opinion was that the legislature becomes a vehicle for the unquestioned exercise of the power of amendment while the dissent insisted that the people in their sovereign capacity alone possesses the amending power and that they may always question legislative power.

The third passage is from *Alcorn* v. *Hamer* where again the high court equated the "state" with the "people constituting the state." That case, it will be remembered, held that there was no unconstitutional delegation of legislative power in a tax measure which, although complete in itself, depended for its actual collection upon the contingency of an affirmative county vote. Building its theory of constitutionality very gradually, the court began as follows:

According to the theory of the government of Mississippi, indeed according to the principles which are universally regarded as fundamental in all the American systems of government, all political power is inherent in the people; and all free government is founded on their authority, and established for their benefit. And hence, that they have an inalienable and indefeasible right to abolish their form of government, or to alter it in such manner as they may deem most conducive to their welfare.

. . . *The sovereign power of this State, or the people in their national or sovereign capacity*, have ordained a Constitution, and by it have established a government, and clothed it with all the powers which it possesses. (Emphasis added.) [33]

[33] 38 Miss. 652, 747–48 (1860).

On a superficial reading, the foregoing three declarations of popular sovereignty appear to be expressions of orthodox American political theory. Yet, when the passages quoted above from *Green* and *Alcorn* are read in the light of the political philosophy of Jefferson Davis, John C. Calhoun, and John A. Quitman, all of whom equated the "people" in their sovereign capacity with the "state," they take on a new meaning. According to Jefferson Davis, "The States *are* the people. The people do not speak, never have spoken, and never can speak, in their sovereign capacity (without a subversion of our whole system), otherwise than as the people of States." [34]

Before Davis, Calhoun had argued that sovereignty resides "in the people of the several States, in their confederated character"; and that "it cannot be found in the people, taken in the aggregate." [35] "The truth is," Calhoun asserted, "that the very idea of an *American People*, as constituting a single community, is a mere chimera." [36]

The creation of the federal government by the states qua states was only a step away. John A. Quitman, congressman from Mississippi from 1855 to 1858 (the year of his death), took

[34] Davis, *Rise and Fall of the Confederate Government*, I, 152. Davis wrote this two-volume work between 1876 and 1881 while in retirement in Beauvoir, Mississippi. It is a conglomeration of his political and constitutional theories, autobiography and personal memoirs, selected letters and public speeches, a history of slavery and the sectional crisis, an account of the Civil War and the trials of the Confederate Government, and an apologia of the Confederate cause. The opening paragraph of the Preface reads:

> The object of this work has been from historical data to show that the Southern States had rightfully the power to withdraw from a Union into which they had, as sovereign communities, voluntarily entered; that the denial of that right was a violation of the letter and spirit of the compact between the States; and that the war waged by the Federal Government against the seceding States was in disregard of the limitations of the Constitution, and destructive of the principles of the Declaration of Independence.

[35] Richard K. Crallé (ed.), *Works of Calhoun*, Vol. I: *Disquisition on Government* (Charleston, S.C.: Steam Power-Press of Walker and James, 1851), hereinafter referred to as Crallé (ed.), *Disquisition on Government*.

[36] Richard K. Crallé (ed.), *Works of Calhoun*, Vol. VI: *Reports and Public Letters* (New York: D. Appleton and Company, 1856), 107.

that step in a speech before the House of Representatives on December 18, 1856:

The Constitution of the United States was acceded to by the states as states. Each for itself, in its sovereign capacity, entered into the compact. We find in it the delegation of some of the powers of government, but no cessions of sovereign power. That rested originally with the states; and there, I contend, it remains today. If it does not rest with the states where is it? I have shown that this government being possessed only of limited powers, for specified purposes, can not be sovereign. That high power, I repeat, remains where it originally rested—in the states of this Union; and whenever it is called into action it must flow from its pristine source.[37]

These political utterances were relatively contemporaneous statements from the states' rights school of political philosophy which had been gathering momentum in Mississippi as the Civil War approached, and there is no evidence that the justices on the Mississippi High Court adhered to any different philosophy. Indeed, the very language quoted from the dissenting opinion in *Green* v. *Weller* refers to "the State, or the people constituting the State, . . . in the plenitude of their sovereignty," [38] explicitly making the Davis equation of "people" with the "State." And when in *Alcorn* v. *Hamer* the court said that "the sovereign power of this State, or the people in their national or sovereign

---

[37] J. F. H. Claiborne, *Life and Correspondence of John A. Quitman* (2 vols.; New York: Harper and Brothers, 1860), II, 342–43. Quitman was a native of New York state, but no more fanatical secessionist ever lived. A lawyer by profession, he settled in Natchez, Mississippi, at the age of twenty-three, and later became identified with a group known as "Nullifiers," who held the views of the nullification leaders of South Carolina. He served in the state senate in 1835 and then in the Mexican War under General Zachary Taylor. Elected governor of Mississippi in 1849, Quitman so vigorously opposed the Compromise of 1850 that even in that year he pressed for unilateral secession by Mississippi, whatever the consequences. In 1851 he ran for governor again on an anti-compromise platform but withdrew his nomination after the election of delegates to the Convention of 1850 resulted in a large Union majority. Speaking on the subject of secession shortly before his death in 1858, Quitman asked the rhetorical question: "What should we have to fear? What army or navy would act against us? Where would the money come from to reduce us to subjection? Our physical power and military spirit are known to the world. . . . It is folly to talk of coercing the South. We laugh at such a threat, as we laugh at the mean and dastardly idea that our slaves would join our assailants." (pp. 268–69)

[38] 32 Miss. 650 (1856).

capacity, have ordained a Constitution," [39] it was finding the same coincidence. Since the *Harry* v. *Decker* decision of 1818, the concept of sovereignty had shifted in meaning from "people" to "state." To be sure, it was the Mississippi politicians, and not the high court, who, in the passages quoted thus far, projected the idea of the states as the embodiment of sovereignty into a theory of the nature and origin of the federal government. However, the court did address itself to that problem in another line of cases to be considered later, and in a manner completely in accord with the Calhoun-Davis-Quitman philosophy.

In the meanwhile, the Supreme Court of the United States was evolving its own ideas of the nature of government and popular sovereignty in the American context. In *Chisholm* v. *Georgia*,[40] the Court took a view quite different from the states' rights school of thought:

> . . . the people, in their collective and national capacity, established the present constitution. It is remarkable that in establishing it, the people exercised their own rights and their own proper sovereignty, and, conscious of the plenitude of it, they declared with becoming dignity, "We, the *people* of the *United States*, do ordain and establish this constitution." Here we see the people acting as sovereigns of the Whole country, and in the language of sovereignty, establishing a constitution by which it was their will that the State Governments should be bound, and to which the State Constitutions should be made to conform . . . ; and the constitution of the *United States* is likewise a compact, made by the people of the *United States* to govern themselves as to general objects, in a certain manner.[41]

And in *Martin* v. *Hunter's Lessee* [42] the Court denied the theory that the Constitution was a creature of the states: "The Constitu-

---

[39] 28 Miss. 652 (1860).

[40] 2 U.S. (2 Dall.) 419 (1793). The Court held that under the Constitution of the United States as adopted, a state could be sued in the United States Supreme Court by a citizen of another state in assumpsit; and, unless the state appeared, judgment by default could be entered. This rule was nullified by the Eleventh Amendment.

[41] *Ibid.*, 470–71.

[42] 14 U.S. (1 Wheat.) 304, 324 (1816). The Court held that the jurisdiction of the United States Supreme Court extends to appellate review of decisions of state courts on questions of federal law.

tion of the United States was ordained and established, not by the States in their sovereign capacities, but emphatically, as the preamble of the Constitution declares, by the 'people of the United States.' "

In *McCulloch* v. *Maryland*,[43] John Marshall made the same point: "The government of the Union, then, is, emphatically, and truly, a government of the people. In form and in substance it emanates from them. Its powers are granted by them, and are to be exercised directly on them, and for their benefit."

Whether, and how far one should interpolate the Mississippi political ambiance into the opinions of its high court depend in some measure on one's own view of the judicial process and its relationship to the political environment. The precise degree of penetration of the states' rights philosophy into the appellate court is hardly a mathematical quantity; in the light of the cases to be considered momentarily, however, the inference of total judicial endorsement of that philosophy is compelling.[44]

A second reading of the three quotations from *Harry* v. *Decker*, *Green* v. *Weller*, and *Alcorn* v. *Hamer* suggests a still more provocative association of ideas. In all three, the notion of popular sovereignty is intimately linked with the correlative idea of the "unalienable" right of the people "to alter or abolish" their government "at will." Both concepts have a common source, derivatively in the Mississippi Constitution of 1832,[45] and ul-

---

[43] 17 U.S. (4 Wheat.) 316, 404–405 (1819). The Court upheld the constitutionality of the act of Congress incorporating the Bank of the United States and denied the power of a state to tax its operations.

[44] One case in this period rested its decision squarely on the rationale of state sovereignty. In Saffarans v. Terry, 20 Miss. (12 S. & M.) 690 (1849) the court held that a sale under execution against an Indian having a reservation under a treaty with the federal government, which forbade the sale of the lands without approval of the president, was valid and passed title to the purchaser without compliance with any of the stipulations of the treaty. To hold otherwise "would be trenching too far on state sovereignty." *Ibid.*, 696.

[45] Miss. Const. art. I, § 2: "That all political power is inherent in the people, and all free governments are founded on their authority, and established for their benefit; and, they have at all times an unalienable and indefeasible right to alter or abolish their form of government, as they may think expedient."

timately in the Declaration of Independence. In a sense, both are legitimate expressions of basic tenets of the American political creed and their association by the Mississippi High Court is not particularly striking, so long as the court was rationalizing at the state level. But once the "state" is held to be the embodiment of sovereignty, the right to "alter or abolish" the government on the *federal* level becomes a right or prerogative of the state rather than the people.[46]

Parenthetically, it is significant that this belief in the right to "alter or abolish" became, with the approach of the Civil War, one of the arguments used to support the act of secession as a revolutionary remedy sanctioned by the Declaration of Independence. Proof of the strong revolutionary flavor surrounding the act and the equally strong desire to legitimize it, is found in the following passage from Jefferson Davis's Inaugural Address to the Confederate Congress shortly before the outbreak of war:

> Our present political position has been achieved in a manner unprecedented in the history of nations. It illustrates the American idea that governments rest on the consent of the governed, and that it is the right to alter or abolish them at will whenever they become destructive of the ends for which they were established. . . . In this [act of secession] they [the Confederate States] merely asserted the right which the Declaration of Independence of July 4, 1776, defined to be "inalienable." Of the time and occasion of its exercise they as sovereigns were the final judges, each for itself.[47]

Yet, Davis's speech did not tell the entire story. The truth is that, even at the moment of withdrawal from the Union on January 9, 1861, Mississippi was ravaged by a tension between two strong but irreconcilable forces which had given the state a double image for ten years—in fact, ever since the Compromise

[46] Calhoun had argued that the reserved powers of the states include the power to alter or abolish the Constitution at the pleasure of the states. See Crallé (ed.), *Disquisition on Government*, 138–39, 274–75.
[47] Davis, *Rise and Fall of the Confederate Government*, I, 232.

of 1850.[48] One held secession to be both peaceable and constitutional; the other, both bloody and rebellious. In 1851, the convention of delegates which convened for the express purpose of either affirming or rejecting the 1850 compromise officially labeled secession as "civil revolution" after a bitter and dramatic struggle between these opposing forces. Mississippi in that year elected to stay in the Union when it became apparent that she would have to go it alone if she chose to secede. Resolution 4 contains the written answer of the state to the Compromise of 1850:

4th, Resolved, further, That, in the opinion of this Convention, the asserted right of secession from the Union on the part of a State or States is utterly unsanctioned by the Federal Constitution, which was framed to "establish" and not to destroy the union of the States, and that no secession, can, in fact, take place without a subversion of the Union established, and which will not virtually amount to its effects and consequences to a civil revolution.[49]

In spite of Resolution 4, however, most Mississippi secessionists were arguing throughout the decade of the 1850s that the "right" to secede was derived from the nature of the federal compact as a league of independent sovereign states, which, in the same manner as they created the Union, could unmake it at will. Each possessed the power to judge infractions of the compact; each had the right peaceably to withdraw when the compact no longer served the purposes for which it was formed. This line of reasoning was, of course, pure Calhoun in a local setting. The more radical Mississippi secessionists, embodied in the figure of John A. Quitman, all but conceded that the act was a rev-

---

[48] Proposed by Henry Clay, the compromise provided for the admission of California to the Union as a free state, the organization of the New Mexico and Utah territories without restriction on slavery, adjustment of the Texas-New Mexico boundary, settlement of the Texas debt, abolition of the slave trade in the District of Columbia, and more stringent fugitive slave laws.

[49] *Journal of the Convention of the State of Mississippi* (Jackson, Miss.: Thomas Palmer, 1851), 47.

olutionary remedy and not a constitutional right, but urged that
the time had come to assert it, whatever the consequences.[50]
And Albert Gallatin Brown, Mississippi's plainspoken United
States senator from 1854 to 1861, went so far as to say on October 18, 1860, that he wanted to "get out of this concern," and he
had neither "the time nor the inclination to discuss the right of
secession." [51]

By January, 1861, the state was hopelessly confused as to
whether its proposed deed was an act of unmitigated rebellion
or the exercise of a peaceable constitutional prerogative. In this
frame of mind, what emerged from the convention of 1861,
called by the legislature "to consider the then existing relation
between the Government of the United States and the Government of the people of the State of Mississippi, and to adopt such
measures for the vindication of the sovereignty of the State and
the protection of its institutions as shall appear to be demanded" [52] were two brief documents: (1) the Declaration of
Causes and (2) the Ordinance of Secession. The declaration,
after reciting the familiar catalog of grievances against the North,
concluded on the following note of resignation and revolution:

[50] "We separated from England for the mere assertion of a right which she was willing to
qualify or surrender, and which had never occasioned any actual evil. When we leave the
present Union, we shall leave it to preserve our property from spoilation, our homesteads
from rapine and murder. We shall stand justified in our own conscience and before
mankind; justified as every people stand justified in history, who, having patiently endured injustice for the sake of peace, finally draw the sword for the sake of independence." Claiborne, *Life and Correspondence of John A. Quitman*, II, 270–71.

[51] A native of South Carolina, Brown moved to Mississippi at the age of ten and began
practicing law at twenty. He entered politics as an ardent Jacksonian Democrat in the
state legislature. After serving a term in Congress, he was elected governor in 1843 and
served two terms. From 1848 to 1854 he served again in the House of Representatives
and from 1854 to 1861 in the United States Senate. He strongly opposed the Compromise of 1850 and believed from that date on that secession was the only remedy for the
south. See M. W. Cluskey (ed.), *Speeches, Messages, and Other Writings of Albert G.
Brown* (2d ed.; Philadelphia: Jas. B. Smith & Company, 1859), 597–99, 604–611, *passim*.
Brown is here quoted in Percy L. Rainwater, *Mississippi: Storm Center of Secession,
1856–1861* (Baton Rouge, La.: Otto Claitor, 1938), 44.

[52] Act of November 28, 1860, ch. 1, § 5, *Laws of Mississippi, Passed at a Called Session*
(Jackson, Miss.: E. Barksdale, State Printer, 1860), 32.

Utter subjugation awaits us in the Union, if we should consent longer to remain in it. It is not a matter of choice, but of necessity. We must either submit to degradation and to the loss of property worth four billions of money, or we must secede from the Union framed by our fathers, to secure this as well as every other species of property. For far less cause than this, our fathers separated from the Crown of England.

Our decision is made. We follow in their footsteps.[53]

The ordinance chose to rely on the resumption by the state of the powers granted to the federal government; that is, the assertion of its constitutional prerogative:

Section 1st. That all the laws and ordinances by which the said State of Mississippi became a member of the Federal Union and the United States of America be, and the same are hereby repealed, and all obligations on the part of the said State or the people thereof to observe the same, be withdrawn, and that the said State doth hereby resume all the rights, functions and powers which, by any of said laws or ordinances, were conveyed to the government of the said United States, and is absolved from all the obligations, restraints and duties incurred to the said Federal Union, and shall from henceforth be a free, sovereign and independent State.[54]

On what theory had the state seceded then? Was it exercising a constitutional right or invoking a revolutionary remedy? Unable to resolve the contradiction, and unable to bear the tension, Mississippi chose to go out clasping both.[55]

[53] *Journal of the Convention, 1861*, 87–88.
[54] *Ibid.*, 119.
[55] An interesting postscript to the theoretical dilemma embedded in the secession convention of 1861 lies in Governor James Alcorn's inaugural address delivered in 1870, at the beginning of his term as first civilian governor since the Civil War. He said:

Secession, I have ever denounced as a fallacy. In casting my lot with my own people in the late war, I did not seek justification behind logical subtleties. When I said in the secession convention, "the Rubicon is crossed, I join the army that moves to Rome," I spoke not as a sophist, after the fashion of Calhoun, but as a rebel, after the fashion of Caesar. I took the step in full view of the fact that it was one of simple rebellion. In the exercise of the right of revolution, I accepted all its risks with my eyes open to the fact that those risks included, in both law and fact, the penalties attaching to treason. And during even the first hour of defeat, when I lay with my people crushed under the heels of thundering armies, I accepted the fact that one end of

To be sure, the Mississippi High Court in the *Green* and *Alcorn* cases was not thinking specifically of either revolution or secession, given the issues before it in those cases. However, if we add to the words "sovereignty" and "state" contained in the dicta of *Green* and *Alcorn* the third word "compact" from cases where the court *was* thinking in federal or in interstate terms, a particular constitutional theory evolves which in the end turned out to be the formula for secession.

In the minds of Hobbes, Locke, and Rousseau, the social contract denoted the transformation of the human condition from a state of nature into a state of society. It was, in the political thought of the constitutional fathers essentially a societal compact, used to explain the origins and legitimacy of government in general. To John C. Calhoun and Jefferson Davis, however, the compact theory of government meant something quite different. The very idea of a social compact in the Locke and Rousseau sense was to Calhoun pure fiction, since the natural state of man is the political state: "As then, there never was such a state as the so-called, state of nature, and never can be, it follows that men, instead of being born in it, are born in the social and political state." [56]

The only true compact, according to Calhoun, was that created by the thirteen original states in adopting and ratifying the Constitution of the United States: "The whole [government], taken together, form a federal community;—a community composed of States united by a political compact;—and not a nation composed of individuals united by what is called, a social compact." [57]

----

the rope around my neck and around their necks had been grasped by the hands of a triumphant conqueror.

Quoted in James Garner, *Reconstruction in Mississippi* (New York: Macmillan Company, 1901), 278.

[56] Crallé (ed.), *Disquisition on Government*, 58.   [57] *Ibid.*, 162.

Jefferson Davis, expounding his theory of government in retirement after the war, followed Calhoun's analysis almost to the line and letter. The opening lines of Chapter 7 in Volume II of his *Rise and Fall of the Confederate Government* suggest the monotony of his theme: "I have habitually spoken of the Federal Constitution as a compact, and of the parties to it as sovereign states." And further in the same chapter: ". . .—it does not require the employment of any particular words in the Constitution—to prove that it [the Constitution] was drawn up as a compact between sovereign States entering into a confederacy with each other, and that they ratified and acceded to it separately severally, and independently." [58]

With this historical-philosophical background in mind, the use of the word "compact" in the opinions of the Mississippi High Court falls into one of two categories existing on two different planes of thought: When the court was thinking on the state level, the Mississippi level, its references to "compact" have the societal meaning given by Rousseau, i.e. the original act of forming organized government. The following passages illustrate this connotation of the term. From *Alcorn v. Hamer:*

The proposition, that the legislature can surrender any portion of the authority with which it is vested, or authorize its exercise by any other body, or by the whole people of the State, is alike repugnant to the spirit and positive provisions of the Constitution. . . . It is opposed to the spirit of the Constitution, which is intended for the equal protection of every party to the social compact, who is entitled to demand under its auspices, "that his rights shall be protected, and that his civil conduct shall only be regulated by the associated wisdom, intelligence, and integrity of the whole representation of the State." [59]

The following is from *Griffin v. Mixon:*

Our Constitution, in its first breath, thus speaks the voice of a free people: "That the general, great, and essential principles of liberty and

[58] Davis, *Rise and Fall of the Confederate Government,* I, 134, 140; II, 86–193, *passim.*
[59] 38 Miss. 652, 749 (1860).

free government, may be recognized and established. WE DECLARE"—
(that is, that there may be no dispute between government and citizen;
that the great and essential rights of each individual member of this
public compact may be *"established" thereby,* and *"recognized"* by
their mutual agents and only depositaries of the general powers of government; *it is declared,* among other things), "that all political power is
inherent in the people, and all free governments are founded on their
authority, and established for their benefit." [60]

When the court was thinking on the interstate and federal
level, however, in terms of the structure and philosophy of the
federal government and the relationship of the states among
themselves, it used "compact" in the Calhoun-Jeffersonian sense
as denoting a league of sovereign states. Consider the following
dicta in this connection. The first is from the case of *Dorsey* v.
Maury,[61] which held, in 1848, that the certificate of a discharge
in bankruptcy by the clerk of the district court of the United
States for the eastern district of Louisiana, under seal of that
court, was inadmissible in evidence in an action brought in Mississippi without the authentication of the clerk's certificate by
the judge. Addressing itself to the larger question of interstate
relations, the court stated: "The several states are each sovereign
and independent, and their relations are those of *foreign states
in close friendship,* in regard to all matters not surrendered to
the general government. But for the act of congress, the judgments of each state would be regarded as foreign judgments in
every other." [62]

The next passage is from *Mitchell* v. *Wells,* an 1859 case holding that a "free woman of color," an emancipated slave and a resident of Ohio, could not take personal property by bequest
under a Mississippi will executed by a Mississippi testator. On
the subject of federal-state and interstate relations the majority
opinion came right to the point: " 'Comity' forbids that a sister

[60] 38 Miss. 424, 439 (1860).   [61] 18 Miss. (10 S. & M.) 298 (1848).
[62] *Ibid.,* 300.

State of this confederacy should seek to introduce into the family of States, as equals or associates, a caste of different color, and of acknowledged inferiority, who, though existing among us at the time of our compact of Union, were excluded from the sisterhood by common consent." [63]

Even the dissenting opinion of Mr. Justice Handy in that case agreed with the majority that the federal government was a compact which could be dissolved at will: "Whilst the confederacy continues, we cannot justify ourselves as a State in violating its spirit and principles, because other States have, in some respects, been false to their duties and obligations. It may justify us in dissolving the *compact*, but not in violating our obligations under it whilst it continues." (Emphasis added.) [64]

And in *Shaw* v. *Brown*, another case from the area of manumission, the holding of the Mississippi High Court was diametrically opposed to the rule of *Mitchell*, but the theory of government espoused in that case was identical. On a similar set of facts, the court in *Shaw* allowed a free Negro emancipated in Ohio to take property by will in Mississippi. In the course of its opinion, it said:

> These rules of general law [comity] certainly lose none of their force when applied to a confederacy of States, united together as are the States of this Union, by a solemn compact for mutual protection, and to promote their common defence and general welfare; but must apply, with peculiar force, to the inhabitants of the several States, whose rights are guaranteed by their constitutions and laws. . . . The States do not derive their rights from the Federal Constitution. They existed before the Constitution, and are superior to it except when limited by it. But the Union formed by the Constitution is founded upon the implied covenant, that the rights of its constituent members, as sovereigns, shall be observed and respected. [65]

The following passages trace the corresponding evolution of federal doctrine on the "compact" theory. *Chisholm* v. *Georgia*

---

[63] 37 Miss. 235, 261 (1859).   [64] *Ibid.*, 286.   [65] 35 Miss. 246, 317 (1859).

used the word in a national frame of reference in its societal meaning: "and the Constitution of the *United States* is likewise a compact, made by the people of the United States to govern themselves as to general objects, in a certain manner." [66]

In *Calder* v. *Bull* [67] the word is used in its societal meaning and corresponds to the Mississippi High Court in *Alcorn* v. *Hamer:* "The people of the *United States* erected their constitutions, or forms of government, to establish justice, to promote the general welfare, to secure the blessings of liberty; and to protect their *persons* and *property* from violence. The purposes for which men enter into society will determine the *nature* and *terms* of the *social* compact." [68]

The language quoted earlier in this chapter from *Martin* v. *Hunter's Lessee* and *McCulloch* v. *Maryland* emphatically denied the compact theory of the federal government in its Jeffersonian sense of a confederation of sovereign states without explicitly using the word "compact."

Only in *Withers* v. *Buckley* [69] did the United States Supreme Court refer, in 1857, to the federal government explicitly as a "compact" of states, but in a context which concerned the relationship among the several states of the Union—not the relationship between the states and the federal government.

Clearly, Congress could exact of the new State the surrender of no attribute inherent in her character as a sovereign independent State, or indispensable to her equality with her sister States, necessarily implied

---

[66] 2 U.S. (2 Dall.) 419, 471 (1793).

[67] 3 U.S. (3 Dall.) 386 (1798). The Court held that a law of Connecticut setting aside a decree of a court of probate and granting a new hearing in a contested will case, with the result that Calder was divested of the real estate in question and Bull got title, was not an ex post facto law prohibited by the United States Constitution.

[68] *Ibid.*, 388.

[69] 61 U.S. (20 How.) 84 (1857). The Court held that a law of Mississippi for improving the navigation of a small stream which emptied into the Mississippi River was not in conflict with the act of Congress admitting Mississippi into the Union, and guaranteeing the free navigation of the Mississippi River.

and guarantied by the very nature of the Federal compact. Obviously, and it may be said primarily, among the incidents of that equality is the right to make improvements in the rivers, water-courses, and high-ways, situated within the State.[70]

But in 1858 in *Ableman* v. *Booth* [71] the Court was again back to the national theory of government as a creation of the people of the several states:

Nor is there anything in this supremacy of the General Government, or the jurisdiction of its judicial tribunals, to awaken the jealousy or offend the natural and just pride of State sovereignty. Neither this Government, nor the powers of which we are speaking, were forced upon the States. The Constitution of the United States, with all the powers conferred by it on the General Government, and surrendered by the States, was the voluntary act of the people of the several States, deliberately done, for their own protection and safety against injustice from one another.[72]

And by 1870, the Civil War having intervened, Justice Bradley, writing a concurring opinion in the *Legal Tender Cases* [73] could say:

The doctrine so long contended for, that the Federal Union was a mere compact of States, and that the States, if they chose, might annul or disregard the acts of the National legislature, or might secede from the Union at their pleasure, and that the General government had no power to coerce them into submission to the Constitution, should be regarded as definitely and forever overthrown. This has been finally effected by the National power, as it had often been before, by overwhelming argument.[74]

[70] *Ibid.*, 93.
[71] 62 U.S. (21 How.) 506 (1858). The Court held that a United States marshall, holding a person in custody under the authority of the United States, need not obey the process of the state court (Wisconsin) for the production of the person demanded by a writ of habeas corpus.
[72] *Ibid.*, 524.
[73] 79 U.S. (12 Wall.) 457 (1870). The Court upheld the constitutionality of the Legal Tender Acts (making treasury notes legal tender for the payment of all debts) when applied to contracts made before and after their passage.
[74] *Ibid.*, 555.

Before the Civil War, then, with the exception of *Withers* v. *Buckley*, which might be explained away by an argument that the particular issue in the case suggested the casual reference to a "Federal compact," no United States Supreme Court case ever argued the Davis-Calhoun compact theory of the federal government in anything approaching the extremity and intensity of the Mississippi High Court in *Dorsey* v. *Maury*, *Shaw* v. *Brown*, or *Mitchell* v. *Wells*. Throughout this entire period of its constitutional history, moreover, the justices of the Mississippi High Court repeatedly used the word "confederation" or "confederacy," which suggests a league of sovereign states, rather than "Union" in referring to the national government.[75]

It is remarkable that, in spite of the political implications of the opinions reviewed, in only one area of law involving two cases examined in this chapter was the concrete decision affected by the political philosophy held by the Mississippi High Court. These two were the emancipation cases of *Shaw* v. *Brown* and *Mitchell* v. *Wells*. It is even more striking that these cases were diametrically opposite in result on the same set of facts, although both explicitly endorsed the same theory of American government as a loose compact or confederacy of independent sovereign states. While *Shaw* held that an emancipated slave in Ohio could take property by bequest in Mississippi, and *Mitchell* held that he could not, it was comity which persuaded the court in *Shaw* to rule as it did, *in spite of* the constitutional doctrine of the high court. When that benign influence was discredited as a guide for decision by the Mississippi High Court in the *Mitchell* case, and with it the entire *Shaw* opinion, the rationale of *Mitchell* was left standing as the authoritative pronouncement of the state court in this area before the Civil War. It was a ratio-

---

[75] Foster v. Alston, 7 Miss. (6 How.) 406, 464 (1842); Mahorner v. Hooe, 17 Miss. (9 S. & M.) 247, 278 (1848); Sarah v. State, 28 Miss. 267, 274 (1854); Shaw v. Brown, 35 Miss. 246, 316, 317 (1858); Mitchell v. Wells, 37 Miss. 235, 261, 264 (1859).

nale which rested squarely on state sovereignty and the compact theory of government.[76]

On a more abstract plane, familiar words which had acquired particular connotations in the lexicon of the United States Supreme Court justices became mere symbols denoting other, quite different concepts as they were incorporated into the Mississippi constitutional idiom. By positing the symbolic term "popular sovereignty" as the major premise, and then translating it into the state idiom in the minor premise, two syllogisms can be derived which fashion a distinct theory of American government.

I. Sovereignty resides in the people.
    The States are the people.
    Therefore, the States are sovereign.
II. Sovereignty is the right to abolish the form of government.
    The form of government is a compact of sovereign states.
    Therefore, the states may abolish the compact.

Such, briefly stated, was the argument for the constitutional right of secession more fully developed in the political arena. In the opinions of the Mississippi High Court it was muted, but consciously present nonetheless.

To invest specific words or phrases with symbolic meanings is dangerous, of course, unless the language will bear the investiture. Where the words stand for concepts generally understood and accepted in a society, the symbolic meaning may be not only permissible but more truthful than the face value of the

---

[76] The rationale is briefly as follows: (1) Mississippi came into the Union under a federal constitution which recognized and sanctioned slavery, and which was adopted by the common consent of all states; (2) Mississippi desires to protect and perpetuate the institution of slavery; (3) The law of a sister state with respect to race has no extraterritorial effect and can vest no rights in a black person in Mississippi; (4) No state is under any obligation to give effect to the laws of any other states prejudicial to its own citizens.

words. Such was the case with "sovereignty," "state," "alter or abolish," "compact," and "confederacy" in the lexicon of Mississippi's political and social order. To speak the words was to invoke an ethos which ended ineluctably, by the force of its own logic, in secession.

CHAPTER II

Was That Contract Impaired?

It was no secret that the state of Mississippi, throughout the three decades before the Civil War, nourished a profound grudge against state banks. Philosophizing on what one observer described as the "national madness," the high court in *Nevitt v. Bank of Port Gibson* [1] lamented the situation in 1846:

> The history of legislation in the states of this Union affords but too many instances of the fatal facility of chartering banks, and too many evidences of the ill effects of such policy. At some period or other of their existence, a great proportion of the states has run the same round which ours has done. Numerous banking companies have been incorporated—excessive issues of their paper have been made—inflation—depreciation and insolvency have followed; and then comes legislation to compel them to wind up, to seize on their charters, and to save a few planks from the wreck. The same general features are exhibited in their course—a course too often "begun in folly, closed in tears." An eloquent advocate describes it as a sort of national madness, insists that no one should be punished for it, and declares that he knows not how to frame a bill of indictment against a whole people. The cool and sagacious sons of New England, the impetuous and impulsive children of the South, and the hardy and adventurous men of the West, have all performed the same circuit. [2]

[1] 14 Miss. (6 S. & M.) 513 (1846).   [2] *Ibid.*, 525.

Twelve years later the court went out of its way to make that antipathy quite clear in its dicta in *Shaw* v. *Brown*, a case having nothing whatsoever to do with banking institutions: "The laws and policy of this State are strongly in opposition to banks. For years past, the legislature has discountenanced the banking system, by refusing to charter new banks, and by passing the most stringent and rigorous laws in relation to those already chartered. The legislative disapprobation of the system is thus shown, and is well understood to be a matter of public policy." [3]

Frontal assaults on the banks had come as early as 1840 in the form of legislation so crippling in its effect that the outcry of the banks eventually reached the Supreme Court of the United States, and brought the state to its first direct confrontation with federal power. The constitutional issue concerned, of course, the impairment of contracts clause of art. I, § 10 of the federal Constitution,[4] a subject on which one might comfortably say that the United States Supreme Court was entitled to speak finally and incontrovertibly. It did so speak in the full plenitude of federal supremacy, even up to the point of holding a portion of Mississippi's legislation unconstitutional. Yet, partly because of an insidious feature imbedded in this issue, and partly because of Mississippi's obduracy in pursuing its war on the banks, the state was able to deflect the impact of the Supreme Court's decision. Whether the high court should be commended for its ingenuity or condemned for its arrogance is to some extent a subjective evaluation rooted in one's particular stance on the question of the proper balance between state and federal power. What is worthy of analysis, however, is the process by which the Missis-

[3] 35 Miss. 246, 319 (1858). The case concerned the manumission of slaves.
[4] This section reads as follows: "No State shall enter into any Treaty, Alliance, or Confederation; grant Letters of Marque and Reprisal; coin Money; emit Bills of Credit; make any Thing but gold and silver Coin a Tender in Payment of Debts; pass any Bill of Attainder, ex post facto Law, or Law impairing the Obligation of Contracts, or grant any Title of Nobility."

sippi High Court was able to preserve intact a legislative measure embracing a tenaciously held state policy, in the face of a flat ruling of unconstitutionality by the Supreme Court of the United States.

The litigation of *Payne* v. *Baldwin*,[5] decided in 1844, opens the story in its judicial setting. A statute enacted four years before had forbidden all state banks from negotiating by endorsement or otherwise any notes, bills, or other evidences of debt.[6] In plain violation of the law a state bank (the Mississippi Railroad Company) transferred two negotiable notes to one Baldwin, the notes bearing the date December 4, 1839.[7] According to the 1840 statute, any action brought upon a note so transferred was to abate. When, therefore, Baldwin as endorsee sued the makers of the notes and the defense of the statute was predictably made, the constitutionality of the act quickly became the sole question before the high court.

While endorsing wholeheartedly the doctrine of *The Dartmouth College Case*,[8] which had held that a charter of a private corporation is a contract within the meaning of the Constitution which a state legislature may not abridge with impunity, the high court nevertheless upheld the Mississippi law. The rationale used by the court was soon to become a familiar one: the bank's contract, or charter, had not been impaired because that charter never authorized the bank to negotiate notes in the first

---

[5] 11 Miss. (3 S. & M.) 661 (1844).

[6] The title of this comprehensive banking statute was "An Act Requiring the Several Banks in this State to pay Specie, and for other purposes," enacted February 21, 1840; ch. 15, § 7, *Hutchinson's Code* (1848), 325. The text of section 7 reads: "It shall not be lawful for any bank in this state to transfer by endorsement or otherwise, any note, bill receivable, or other evidence by debt; and if it shall appear in evidence, upon the trial of any action upon any such note, bill receivable, or other evidence of debt that it was so transferred, the same shall abate upon the plea of the defendant."

[7] The notes were executed by a certain Payne who had discounted them at the bank on the date of execution. The bank (Mississippi Railroad Company) subsequently became indebted to Baldwin and negotiated the two notes to him in payment of the debt.

[8] 17 U.S. (4 Wheat.) 518 (1819).

place. By interpreting the provisions of the underlying contract narrowly, so as to exclude from its terms the conduct prohibited by the subsequent legislation, the court was able to circumvent the federal contract clause.

Undoubtedly it came as a shock to the bank to learn that a practice which was by that time customary in the banking business was not conferred by its charter, but rather that the power to negotiate notes had come as a legislative dispensation. On this point the court was most emphatic:

With us they [bills and notes] derive the character of negotiability from a statute, which declares, that all bonds, notes, &c., may be assigned by indorsement, and the indorsee may maintain an action in his own name, and recover, subject however to offsets acquired before notice of transfer. Now let us sweep this statute from the statute book, and suppose that no such law had ever existed, could any one imagine in such a case, that this bank charter made notes negotiable by indorsement, and enabled the holder to sue in his own name and recover? Does it perform the office of the statute of Anne and of our own statute, and enable the bank, in the legal and mercantile sense of the term, to assign its notes by indorsement? To these questions there can be but one answer, and that in the negative.[9]

It followed that the power once conferred could be taken away by the dispenser:

Negotiability is an incident or quality attached to notes by law, not by the charter. It does not constitute an essential ingredient in a note. It does not strengthen the contract between the maker and payee, nor does it constitute any part of that contract; and as it was a privilege enjoyed by the corporation solely under the general law, it is one which was taken from them by the repeal of the law. The charter gives them no guaranty that the law should not be repealed. It was a subject over which the legislature had entire control when the charter was granted, and this, like all other subjects, is still subject to that control, unless a clear and positive restriction has been imposed.[10]

However adroit this rationale, the narrow holding of the case remained that the endorsee, Baldwin, could not sue on the

[9] 11 Miss. (3 S. & M.) at 678.   [10] Ibid., 680.

notes in his own name. What if the action had been brought by the bank? Would the court go so far as to deny *anyone* the right to sue before, as well as after, an illegal transfer? This question the court had to face in *Planters Bank* v. *Sharp*.[11] Here the bank began suit on the notes *before* the transfer. There was nothing on the face of the declaration to show that an assignment had been made. In analyzing this question the majority of the court conceded that the policy behind the act, i.e., "to enable the debtors of the bank under all circumstances to pay their debts in the notes of the banks," seemed to dictate that "the case would appear not to fall within the reason of the law." Yet, the court denied the right of the bank to maintain the action on the ground that the language of the statute was "too plain to admit of more than one construction."[12] Since the act declared that the action shall abate upon the plea of the defendant if it appeared *at the trial* that a transfer had been made, and since the defendant had pleaded the transfer by way of defense (*puis darrein continuance*),[13] that was sufficient reason, in the opinion of the high court, for entering a judgment in abatement.[14]

Chief Justice Sharkey dissented. He regarded the statute "not as a punishment on the bank, by compelling a forfeiture of its right of action, but as intended solely and exclusively for the benefit of bank debtors." An assignment made *after* suit was, in the view of the chief justice, merely a transfer of the proceeds of the suit. In an action by the bank, the endorsee would have no power to vary defendant's right to offsets, and the act applied logically only to cases in which suit was brought in the name of the endorsee. Sharkey noted:

Bank paper was then generally very much depreciated, and the country was full of this depreciated currency, and it was designed to

[11] 12 Miss. (4 S. & M.) 3 (1844).   [12] *Ibid.*, 27.
[13] The name of a plea which a defendant is allowed to put in, after having already pleaded, where some new matter of defense arises after the issue is joined.
[14] Planters Bank v. Sharp, 12 Miss. (4 S. & M.) 3, 27 (1844).

secure to debtors the right to pay the banks in their own notes. By allowing them to transfer their notes, debtors would have been compelled to pay the indorsees in the constitutional currency. But when the suit is brought in the name of the bank, this difficulty cannot occur. An assignee can then have no control of the matter.[15]

These two cases were eventually to reach the United States Supreme Court. In the meanwhile, however, the state legislature continued its vendetta on the banks, giving rise to a series of four cases decided between 1844 and 1847 in the Mississippi High Court, all addressing themselves to the constitutionality of various pieces of restrictive legislation. Without indulging in their highly technical details, a synopsis of these four cases will illustrate the extent to which the legislature controlled, or attempted to control, the banks of Mississippi by 1846.

1. *Commercial Bank* v. *State* [16] upheld section 6 of the act of 1843, which prescribed a mode of proceeding against banks for a violation of their charters. That act authorized, upon the filing of a quo warranto proceeding by the state for forfeiture of the bank's charter, an injunction as a matter of right, restraining the bank from collecting any obligations claimed by it during the pendency of the proceedings in quo warranto.[17] The court found nothing in the charter itself which gave a bank the right to enjoy its franchise until dissolved by judgment. Furthermore, it reasoned that the injunction merely "suspended" a remedy; it did not take away the *right* of suit. Thus, the bank theoretically could still sue, but it could not collect.

2. *Nevitt* v. *Bank of Port Gibson* upheld three other sections of the same act of 1843 (§§ 8, 9, and 10), which provided, in substance, that after a judgment of forfeiture has been entered against a bank, its debtors should not be released from their debts and liabilities, but that the court should appoint trustees to take over the assets, sue for and collect all debts due the

[15] *Ibid.*, 28–29.   [16] 12 Miss. (4 S. & M.) 439 (1845).
[17] Act of July 26, 1843, ch. 15, § 6, *Hutchinson's Code* (1848), 329.

bank, and apply the same to the payment of its debts.[18] It should be noted that, at the time of incorporation of the Bank of Port Gibson, the law in Mississippi followed the common-law rule and allowed a debtor to be released from his liability upon a forfeiture of the bank's charter. Tossing aside the contention that the existing state law formed a part of the contract which could not be impaired by the sate, the high court reasoned that the decision in the *Commercial Bank* case virtually compelled a ruling of constitutionality in the case at bar. Since the various provisions of the act of 1843 were inextricably related, they had to stand or fall together. Therefore, once the *Commercial Bank* case had upheld the constitutionality of section 6, authorizing the injunction during forfeiture proceedings, that decision determined the outcome of future challenges to subsequent sections of the act.

3. In the same year, *Commercial Bank* v. *State* [19] passed on section 8 of the act of 1840 which required all banks in the state to resume specie payments on their notes of various denominations at stated intervals or forfeit their charters.[20] The Commercial Bank of Natchez, along with most state banks, was in a state of suspension of specie payments at the time this act was passed and could not comply. In the forfeiture proceedings initiated under the 1843 law, the bank challenged the validity of section 8. Again the high court examined the charter itself to find whether it had been violated by the 1840 statute, and decided that it had not, the duty to redeem in specie being a "condition in the charter." [21] Observe how the court adroitly skirted the constitutional question:

But it [section 8] is said to be unconstitutional, because it imposes duties and obligations repugnant to the provisions of the charter. We

[18] Act of July 26, 1843, ch. 15, §§ 8–10, *Hutchinson's Code* (1848), 330–31.
[19] 14 Miss. (6 S. & M.) 599 (1846). The bank involved in this litigation was the Commercial Bank of Natchez.
[20] Act of February 21, 1840, ch. 15, § 8, *Hutchinson's Code* (1848), 325.
[21] 14 Miss. (6 S. & M.) at 622.

recognize the doctrine to its full extent, that an act of incorporation is a contract within the meaning of the constitution of the United States, and that any legislative act which impairs it by enlarging the power of the state over the body corporate, or by abridging the franchises, or which alters it in any material point, is void; but no such effect is perceived as resulting from this act. We have said that it was necessarily a condition in the charter, a paramount duty, that the bank should redeem its notes with specie; we have also said that it acquired no right to refuse to redeem in consequence of the right given to the noteholder to demand interest. If these positions be correct, it follows that it was always the duty of the bank to redeem. The state made no contract by which the bank could be excused from the performance of this duty. This act then superadds no new duty or obligation. It does not enlarge the power of the state; it does not diminish any power or privilege of the bank; it does not add to or vary the charter in the slightest degree to the prejudice of the bank. It only requires that to be done by express terms, which the bank was before impliedly bound to do. It was a command that the bank should by a certain day perform the condition of its contract.[22]

4. Buoyed by these three cases upholding its crusade against the banks, the legislature then committed the sin of pride. It passed in 1846 a law amending the act of 1843 to provide that the trustees appointed under the 1843 law should *sell* to the highest bidder, for cash, all the property and evidences of debt of banks whose charters were declared forfeited, the proceeds of the sale to be distributed among the creditors.[23] This act was held unconstitutional in *Commercial Bank* v. *Chambers* [24] on the ground that it impaired the rights of creditors which had vested under the 1843 law. By that act a trust for their benefit was raised, which, once created, could not be taken away by the state.

The stage was now set for the erosion of the still formidable legislative structure by the Supreme Court of the United States. By 1848 the companion cases of *Planters' Bank* v. *Sharp* [25] and

[22] *Ibid.*, 622–23.
[23] Act of February 28, 1846, ch. 15, §§ 1–5, *Hutchinson's Code* (1848), 332.
[24] 16 Miss. (8 S. & M.) 2 (1847).   [25] 47 U.S. (6 How.) 301 (1848).

Baldwin v. *Payne* [26] had found their way up to the nation's highest tribunal, where the question was squarely posited whether the Mississippi statute of 1840 prohibiting state banks from negotiating their bills and notes did impair the obligation of contract between the banks and the state. In deciding that question affirmatively the Court departed radically from the rationale used in the two opinions written by the Mississippi justices. Not only did the charter itself grant to the banks the right to negotiate their notes, but such a right was also found to be an "incident to its business as a bank"; and even essential in some instances, to sound banking:

It may, to be sure, independent of justifications like these, not be customary for banks to dispose of their notes often. But in exigencies of indebtedness and other wants under pressures like those referred to, it may not only be permissible, but much wiser and safer to do it than to issue more of its own paper, too much of it being already out, or part with more of its specie on hand, too little being now possessed for meeting all its obligations. Indeed, its right to sell any of its property, when not restricted in the charter or any previous law, is perhaps as unlimited as that of an individual, if not carried into the transaction of another separate and unauthorized branch of business. [27]

Having ascertained the extent of the contract made by the state with the bank in the charter, the Court turned to examine the scope of the contract between the maker of the note and the bank: "This contract, then, by the bank with the maker, when executed, enabled the former to sell or assign it, and the indorsee to collect it, not only by its express terms but by the general law of the State, then allowing transfers of negotiable paper and suits in the name of indorsees." [28]

The only remaining subject of inquiry was the effect of the 1840 law on these two contracts. By expressly taking away the right of the bank to make any transfer whatever of its notes and

[26] 47 U.S. (6 How.) 332 (1848).
[27] Planters' Bank v. Sharp, 47 U.S. (6 How.) 301, 322–23 (1848).   [28] *Ibid.*, 324.

by virtually depriving an assignee of the notes of the right to sustain any suit, either in his own name or that of the bank, to recover against the maker, that law "vitally changed the obligation of the contract between him and the bank, to pay any assignee of it, as well as changed the obligation of the other contract between the State and the bank in the charter, to allow such notes to be taken and transferred." [29]

In commenting on the policy underlying the law the Court suggested that its design and purpose (to insure billholders of the bank, when debtors, the privilege of paying in the bills of the bank) could have been accomplished by providing that promissory notes, even though assigned by banks, should still be open to setoffs by their debtors of any of their bills which they then held. The Court continued:

> But instead of resorting to such measures, the legislature adopted a shorter and more sweeping mode of attaining the end of preventing assignments which might embarrass or defeat set-offs. They did it by cutting off all assignments whatever, and all remedies whatever upon them. And they accompanied this by another statute, enabling debtors of the bank who held its notes, when their debts fell due, to pay in them, or set them off, and even virtually authorized them to make payment in depreciated bills or notes afterwards bought up for that purpose, and thus to gain an undue advantage over set-offs by other debtors in other matters.
> . . . These two acts, though undoubtedly well meant, and designed to give an honest preference to bill-holders [see Sharkey's dissenting opinion] as to a paper currency which ought always to be kept on a par with specie, were unfortunately, in the laudable zeal to avert a great apprehended evil, passed, without sufficient consideration of the limitations of the powers imposed by the Constitution of the Union on the state legislatures, not to impair the obligation of existing contracts. [30]

Without extended analysis the Court reached the same result of unconstitutionality in the twin case of *Baldwin* v. *Payne*. It remained to be seen what course of action Mississippi would

[29] *Ibid.*, 326.   [30] *Ibid.*, 329.

take in future cases arising under the 1840 law now found to be in violation of the United States Constitution.

The first to arise was a quo warranto proceeding brought in 1848 against the Grand Gulf Railroad and Banking Company specifically to test the validity of a general assignment of assets made by that bank after the act of 1840. Whether the trustees appointed by the trial court in the proceeding below or the assignees under the general assignment were entitled to the assets of the bank was the concrete question before the high court in *Grand Gulf R.R.* v. *State.* The court held that the trustees could take only what did not pass by the deed of assignment, albeit with a nostalgic glance at its earlier construction of the act of 1840:

Under the construction of the act of 1840, prohibiting assignments by the banks, heretofore placed upon it by this court, such assignment was void. But the supreme court of the United States has reversed the decision of this court upon that point, on the ground that the act of 1840 was unconstitutional. In cases of that character, that court bears the relation of an appellate tribunal to this, and we feel bound to conform to its construction of the constitution of the United States, when made upon direct appeal from this court.[31]

Montgomery v. *Galbraith* [32] quickly followed on virtually the same facts and in the same posture. Again the court decided in favor of the assignees, citing the United States Supreme Court case of *Baldwin* v. *Payne,* and tersely stating that "we have since conformed to their decision." [33]

Ten years later, in 1858, came a dramatic *volte-face.* The case of *McIntyre* v. *Ingraham* [34] resurrected the old facts of *Payne* v. *Baldwin:* an assignee of a promissory note negotiated to him by the Grand Gulf Bank after passage of the act of 1840 was now suing the maker on the note. Given the Supreme Court decision of *Planters' Bank* v. *Sharp* and its own two rulings in

[31] 18 Miss. (10 S. & M.) 428, 434 (1848).   [32] 19 Miss. (11 S. & M.) 555 (1848).
[33] 19 Miss. at 574.   [34] 35 Miss. 25 (1858).

Montgomery v. *Galbraith* and *Grand Gulf R.R.* v. *State*, no conservative Mississippi lawyer would have wagered on the maker of the note prevailing over the assignee, even less would he have advised his client (the maker) to plead the defense of the unconstitutional statute of 1840. Or *was* it unconstitutional?

In a startling opinion, which must have sent tremors throughout the banking world, the high court held that no right of assignment had been granted in the bank's charter and none could be claimed by implication—precisely the rationale used in *Payne* v. *Baldwin* back in 1844. This time, however, the court had to overcome the strenuous argument made by counsel for the assignee that the act of 1840 had been held unconstitutional by the Supreme Court of the United States and that its decision was conclusive of the judgment in the case at bar. Here is how the court met that argument:

That decision [*Planters' Bank* v. *Sharp*] has been yielded to by this court in the cases in which it was made, and might be considered as conclusive of the question of the constitutionality of the statute in question, as it affected the charters of the particular banks there brought under consideration. But it only declares the statute unconstitutional as to those charters, and we cannot admit its obligatory force as applicable to the present case, and will briefly state the reasons why we do not consider it conclusive of this case.

In the first place, it is only the principle declared in that case that can be considered as applicable to the charter presented for our construction in this case; and we do not recognize the right of any other judicial tribunal, either to expound the statutes of this State, and to determine their legal construction or effect, or to prescribe rules by which we are to be bound in their construction, with the single exception of a statute alleged to be in conflict with the Constitution of the United States. The Supreme Court of the United States is authorized by the 25th section of the Judiciary Act of 1789, to decide the question of the *"validity of the statute of any state, on the ground of its being repugnant to the Constitution of the United States;"* and, of course, the judgment of that court, pronouncing a State statute unconstitutional, as impairing the obligation of a particular contract, will be conclusive upon the State court, upon the *sole question of the effect and character of the statute presented for consideration.* But we deny the power of that court to expound another statute [charter] not alleged to be unconstitutional, and to fix its construction and legal effect in opposition to the adjudications of the State court having jurisdiction of the question, because a particular construction may be attempted to be given to the original statute [charter] by the party complaining, and in order to render the second statute unconstitutional.[35]

The high court was drawing a hairline distinction between the charter of the Planters' Bank (scrutinized in *Planters' Bank* v. *Sharp*) and the charter of the Grand Gulf Railroad and Banking Company (the bank involved in the present litigation). It found that the words in the latter charter giving the Grand Gulf Banking Company the power to *"purchase* and *possess personal estate* of any kind whatever and to sell and dispose of the same at pleasure"* were more restrictive than the corresponding phrase in the charter of the Planters' Bank, *"to receive, retain,* and enjoy *effects of whatever kind* and to dispose of the same." Negotiability might be included within "effects" but not within "personal estate." [36] In this fine discrimination lay the crux of the case, for unless the two charters were seen to contain different grants, the *Planters' Bank* case would be controlling. By the stratagem of examining the underlying contract in every case arising under a law held unconstitutional by the United States Supreme Court, the Mississippi court limited the scope of *Planters' Bank* to the immediate parties, and for all practical purposes squelched it.

As if to underscore its point, the high court in *McIntyre* expounded upon it further:

The nature and extent of the right under the contract depend upon the law of the State, and must be determined by its own tribunals, which furnish the rule of decision upon that point, in cases of this kind, as in all other cases depending upon the construction of the laws of any State. That is a distinct question from the question whether the right

[35] *Ibid.,* 56–57. [36] *Ibid.,* 61.

secured is impaired by the statute alleged to impair it, and is to be determined by reference to the settled law of the State, and not by the views of the Supreme Court upon the subject. And any other doctrine would be in opposition to established principle, subversive of the rightful authority of the State tribunals to interpret their own laws, and to determine the effect of contracts made under them, and productive of conflict between the rules declared by the Supreme Court, and by this court, upon a subject most clearly within our exclusive jurisdiction.[37]

Yet this power or right of the state to determine in the final analysis the "nature and extent of the right under the contract" was precisely what the United States Supreme Court denied it in *Planters' Bank* v. *Sharp:* "The rights of a party under a contract might improperly be narrowed or denied by a State court, without any redress, if their decision on the extent of them cannot be reviewed and overruled here in cases of this kind." [38]

Even more explicit on this point was the United States Supreme Court in 1877, speaking in an opinion [39] which denied the Louisiana Supreme Court the right to interpret an underlying contract with finality, so as to preclude the Supreme Court from reviewing that obligation when measured by the contract clause of the federal Constitution:

. . . this court has always jealously asserted the right, when the question before it was the impairing of the obligation of a contract by State legislation, to ascertain for itself whether there was a contract to be impaired. If it were not so, the constitutional provision could always be evaded by the State courts giving such construction to the contract, or such decisions concerning its validity, as to render the power of this court of no avail in upholding it against unconstitutional legislation.[40]

Thus the Mississippi High Court, in 1858, not only defied the Supreme Court to speak as the final arbiter on questions of federal constitutional law, but in doing so it wrote off by a process of misconstruction two of its own opinions which had attempted to follow the United States Supreme Court. Indeed, the high

---

[37] *Ibid.*, 60–61.   [38] 47 U.S. (6 How.) 301, 327 (1848).
[39] Delmas v. Insurance Co., 81 U.S. (14 Wall.) 661 (1871).   [40] *Ibid.*, 668.

court was less than honest in squaring away *Montgomery* v. *Galbraith* and *Grand Gulf R.R.* v. *State*. When confronted in *McIntyre* v. *Ingraham* with the cogent argument that these two cases had already recognized the binding authority of the Supreme Court's decision, it chose to misread them by stating that the question of the validity of an assignment was never presented in those cases, but rather, "the question for decision was, whether the judgment of forfeiture against the bank for violation of its charter, was correct." [41] This ignores the following statement in *Montgomery* v. *Galbraith:* "The case thus presents the question of the validity of an assignment made by a bank, since the prohibitory act of 1840." [42]

Now to pose an interesting question: suppose that the case of *McIntyre* v. *Ingraham* had been taken up to the Supreme Court of the United States which scrutinized for itself, as it did in *Planters' Bank* v. *Sharp,* the charter of the Grand Gulf Banking Company. Suppose further that the Court construed that charter to embrace the power of the Grand Gulf Banking Company to negotiate its paper; and, repeating the familiar story of the *Planters' Bank* case, held the act of 1840 (which took away that right) unconstitutional for a second time. What could the Mississippi court have done about it? With respect to the *McIntyre* case, obviously nothing. Just as it had to capitulate to the decision in *Planters' Bank* v. *Sharp,* so it would have had to submit to a holding of unconstitutionality in this hypothetical appeal, even though the United States Supreme Court construed the underlying charter differently from the Mississippi High Court. Once this truth is appreciated—a truth which the Mississippi court refused to face—the language in *McIntyre* asserting the right of the state to pass with finality upon its own contracts becomes not only empty bravado, but false constitutional doctrine. Yet, that bravado and doctrine served the immediate pur-

[41] 35 Miss. 25, 62 (1858).   [42] 19 Miss. (11 S. & M.) at 574.

pose of retaining in almost undiminished force throughout the
state an act which most observers might have guessed was con-
signed to the void where unconstitutional acts go, as a result of
the *Planters' Bank* decision.

The more interesting question is what *would* the Mississippi
High Court have done in the future after a second decision of
unconstitutionality? Quite determinedly, it would have waited
for the next attack on the statute of 1840 by another bank, and
then proceeded to narrow the meaning of *its* charter in order to
escape the stigma of unconstitutionality. Furthermore, in view
of the language of the high court in *McIntyre*, it is highly probable that that court would even have construed an identical
charter contrarily to the construction of the United States Supreme Court in *Planters' Bank* v. *Sharp*. (This follows from the
reasoning of *McIntyre* that "the nature and extent of the right
under the contract depend upon the law of the State and must
be determined by its own tribunals." [43]) Such a case would be,
of course, the extreme but not at all inconceivable. Unfortunately for this study, however, it never arose and there were no
more appeals, the banks perhaps not being strong enough for
the task. The Mississippi statute of 1840 remained standing until
it dropped out of the Revised Code of 1857 and the proud stance
of the high court went unrebuked.

Admittedly, the law of negotiable instruments provides rather
dull fare as the raw ingredient out of which to build a constitutional drama having as its theme the struggle over the contract
clause and as its protagonists the United States Supreme Court
and the Mississippi High Court. Yet, the legal technicalities incident to the law of commercial paper should neither over-
shadow the larger picture, nor prevent the drawing of a moral or
two. If nothing else, the study reveals the tremendous resistant
force which a powerfully held state policy can exert in the face of

[43] 35 Miss. at 60.

a direct collision with the federal Constitution. Second, it throws into relief the instrumental role played by a state appellate court in implementing and preserving that policy. Third, at the microscopic level, it exposes the technical virtuosity of the Mississippi High Court as it struggled to limit the flawed statute to the facts and parties of a particular case.

Even after drawing these conclusions one feels that there is still something unresolved, something unfinished about the drama. If there could only be another decision from the United States Supreme Court to come crashing down on Mississippi in order to chastise it for insubordination. Alas, so long as the adversary system of justice prevails, and so long as the Supreme Court sits under the present Constitution,[44] such untidy endings will occur.

---

[44] The reference is to the jurisdictional requirement that only actual "cases and controversies" involving bona fide litigants are heard by the Supreme Court. Until such a case is brought before the Court, it does not pass on constitutional questions arising in state courts.

CHAPTER III

Discord Over
the Directory Clause

In the Mississippi constitution of 1817 appeared the following words midway in the article entitled, quite simply, "Slaves": "They [the general assembly] shall have full power to prevent slaves from being brought into this state as merchandise." No prohibitive legislation of a general character was passed under that grant of power, and traffic in slaves accordingly prospered at a staggering rate.[1]

Significantly, the corresponding article of the constitution of 1832 contained the following provision: "The introduction of slaves into this state as merchandise, or for sale, shall be prohibited from and after the first day of May, 1833."

The authors of that deceptively simple language did not realize that the Supreme Court of the United States and the Mississippi High Court would become hopelessly divided as to its meaning; and, since neither was ever able to convince the other of the soundness of its own argument, two constructions stood firm and fast to the last, each indestructible within its own jurisdiction, each court convinced of the heresy committed by the

---

[1] A statute of 1822 did require vendors of slaves to record certificates of good character at the time of sale; it also forbade convict slaves and African-born slaves from being introduced into the state. In 1820 the slave population of Mississippi was about 33,000; in 1830 it had increased to 65,000; and in 1840, to over 195,000.

other. Eventually the Civil War made anachronisms of both.

In order to appreciate the richer meaning of the judicial struggle over this particular clause, however, the reader must first understand a contradiction between the constitutional prohibition and the entire legal and social order of slaveholding Mississippi. The civil law of the state regarded slaves for most purposes as a "species of property common in this country," [2] and therefore subject to the rules of law governing chattels. (Although the law of Mississippi considered slaves to be personal property, this was not universally true in all the slaveholding states. For example, in Louisiana slaves were treated as immovable property.) "Color," said Chief Justice Sharkey in 1846, "is *prima facie* evidence of servitude. It is *prima facie* evidence of property in someone." [3] As perfunctorily as adjudicating property rights in horses and mules, the justices of the high court ground out over the years a voluminous body of cases governing the law of property applicable to slaves.[4] Besides constituting the everyday subject matter of an infinite number of contracts of sale, whether sold absolutely [5] or conditionally,[6] and whether

[2] Lewis's Adm'rs v. Farrish, 2 Miss. (1 How.) 547, 549 (1837), holding that on proof of a sale of a Negro woman in 1832, the law would presume some value of the Negro in the absence of proof of the actual price.

[3] Thornton v. Demoss, 13 Miss. (5 S. & M.) 609, 618 (1846). The case held that the record of a proceeding by habeas corpus before a circuit judge, in which proceeding a Negro was held to be a free man, was incompetent evidence to overcome the presumption of slavery, on the ground that there was only one statutory method for removing the presumption and establishing freedom. Therefore, the Negro at issue could be levied on by the sheriff.

[4] The high court in Shewalter v. Ford, 34 Miss. 417, 422 (1857), in holding that a warranty of fitness of a slave excludes obvious defects, said: "The rule, however in relation to obvious defects, applies to such imperfections as are plain and palpable, and cannot but be perceived and understood to their full extent by the purchaser, such as the want of a leg, or an arm, or a hand by a slave, or a tail or an ear by a horse."

[5] Barksdale v. Elam, 30 Miss. 694 (1856), holding that title to slaves vests absolutely in the buyer where the seller attempted to impose an illegal condition on the buyer in the contract of sale.

[6] Mount v. Harris, 9 Miss. (1 S. & M.) 185 (1843), holding that a sale of a Negro girl, coupled with an agreement to return her to the vendor if the purchase money be not paid by a given time, is a conditional, and not an absolute sale.

with or without a bill of sale,[7] slaves could be mortgaged,[8] levied upon by creditors,[9] recovered in actions of detinue [10] and replevin,[11] made the subject of larceny,[12] and constituted the res of trusts.[13] They could be hired for a term,[14] bequeathed for life and in remainder,[15] warranteed for title [16] and soundness,[17] and held as tenants in common.[18] In short, except for the area of emancipation (which will be considered separately), there were virtually no limitations on the right to acquire, hold, or dispose of slaves on whatever terms the parties chose.

Yet the fact that slaves were, in some contexts and for some

[7] Conger v. Robinson, 12 Miss. (4 S. & M.) 210 (1845), holding that no bill of sale was necessary to pass title to slaves or any other sale of personal property. Carter v. Burris, 18 Miss. (10 S. & M.) 527 (1848), holding that a bill of sale of a slave may be proven orally to be a mere mortgage.

[8] Harmon v. Short, 16 Miss. (8 S. & M.) 433 (1847), holding that a bona fide purchaser prevails over the mortgagee, where mortgager retained possession of the slave.

[9] Thornton v. Demoss, 13 Miss. (5 S. & M.) 609 (1846).

[10] Jennings v. Gibson, 1 Miss. (Walk.) 234 (1826).

[11] Curll v. Compton, 22 Miss. (14 S. & M.) 56 (1850).

[12] Coon v. State, 21 Miss. (13 S. & M.) 246 (1849); and Randal v. State, 12 Miss. (4 S. & M.) 349 (1845), both holding that a runaway slave may be the subject of larceny.

[13] Fairly Adm'rs v. Fairly, 38 Miss. 280 (1859), holding that a cestui may maintain the legal action of detinue against the trustee for the possession of slaves; Newman v. Montgomery, 6 Miss. (5 How.) 742 (1841), holding that the trustee may sue in detinue to recover possession from the cestui.

[14] Young v. Thompson, 11 Miss. (3 S. & M.) 129 (1844), holding that a hirer of a slave is not liable to the owner of the slave if he absconds during the term unless the hirer caused him to abscond by mistreatment; Trotter v. McCall, 26 Miss. 410 (1853), holding that a hirer of a slave comes under an implied obligation to treat the slave with such care and moderation as an ordinarily prudent man would use toward his own slave.

[15] Judge of Probate v. Alexander, 31 Miss 297 (1856), holding that the issue of a female slave, born during the existence of a tenancy for life in her, goes to the remainderman upon the death of the life tenant.

[16] Long v. Hickingbottom, 28 Miss. 772 (1855), holding that a warranty of title is implied where a seller of a slave in his possession sells him for a fair price; Noel v. Wheatly, 30 Miss. 181 (1855), holding that the amount of damages which the purchaser of a slave is entitled to recover from his vendor for breach of a warranty of title, is the purchase-money and interest, and his expenses incurred in defending the title; he cannot recover for the loss of a good bargain.

[17] Kinley v. Fitzpatrick, 5 Miss. (4 How.) 59 (1839), holding that any language by the vendor which amounts to an affirmation that the property is sound, is a good warranty; Houston v. Burney, 10 Miss. (2 S. & M.) 583 (1844), holding that a warranty of soundness may be proved by parol evidence.

[18] Hinds v. Terry, 1 Miss. (Walk.) 80 (1820), holding that one tenant in common of a slave cannot maintain an action of trover against the other.

purposes, a *unique* species of personal property could not be gainsaid. Occasionally, a particular justice would recognize their uniqueness in the form of mild sarcasm, as did Justice Childs in *Jennings* v. *Gibson,* where he commented: "The citizens of these [slaveholding] states, possessing a species of property, combining some degree of intelligence, with peculiar facilities of exercising the power of locomotion, have frequently resorted to this form of action, [detinue] as being considered a more adequate remedy than the action of trover." [19]

In dicta, the high court remarked in 1844 that "a court of chancery will not interfere to prevent a sale of personal property, unless it be of some peculiar character, as slaves, or have some particular value by reason of which damages might not afford an adequate compensation for its loss." [20] More to the point, slavetraders were not included within the general tax on "transient vendors of merchandise," [21] on the theory that the legislature historically taxed slaves in explicit terms. Creditors could not levy on slaves if there was any other personal property out of which to satisfy the judgment,[22] and, "from the peculiar character of slave property," the high court held in 1843 that a bill in equity would lie to recover them in specie.[23] Then, too, there was the problem of offspring of slaves, necessitating the creation of special rules.[24] Finally, while slaves constituted the subject matter of larceny, they themselves could also commit

---

[19] 1 Miss. (Walk.) 234, 238 (1826).
[20] Beatty v. Smith, 10 Miss. (2 S. & M.) 567, 570 (1844). The case held that equity would not interfere to prevent a sale of cotton.
[21] James v. Elder, 23 Miss. 134 (1851).   [22] Brian v. Davidson, 25 Miss. 213 (1852).
[23] Murphy v. Clark, 9 Miss. (1 S. & M.) 221 (1843). Chief Justice Sharkey dissented from this view in Butler v. Hicks, 19 Miss. (11 S. & M.) 78 (1848). In his opinion, not *every* slave possessed that degree of uniqueness requisite to equity jurisdiction.
[24] Turnbull v. Middleton, 1 Miss. (Walk.) 413 (1831), holding that the issue of mortgaged slaves born after forfeiture of the terms of the mortgage are not subject to the lien under the mortgage; Judge of Probate v. Alexander, 31 Miss. 297 (1856), holding that a bequest of a female slave does not of itself carry the title to her issue, born before the death of the testator.

larceny, in which case the master was liable for the full value of the property stolen.[25]

The very facility, however, which the law of personal property displayed in adjudicating property rights to particular slaves exposed the vulnerability of a state policy which maintained and protected the institution while it attempted to inhibit a form of commerce in the specific commodity. At the heart of the matter lay a question which fairly defied an answer: If slavery were the beneficent institution slaveholders believed it to be, even for the slaves, and if slaves were just a "species of property," why was it necessary to insert a provision in the constitution of 1832 prohibiting their importation as merchandise? In other words, why not accord slaves *all* the attributes of personal property? Private interests naturally encouraged importation for monetary gain; the constitution of 1832 explicitly demanded suppression of the slave traffic in the public interest. As the interpreter of the state constitution, the Mississippi High Court inevitably found itself in the uncomfortable position of defending a public policy which denied to slavevendors a right enjoyed by all other merchants of chattels—the right to import their wares for resale.

One motivating factor behind the constitutional prohibition was, of course, the desire to soothe the public conscience, which by 1832 had become disquieted over the evils and abuses attending traffic in blacks. It was time to draw a line between the good slaveholder and the bad slavevendor. Speaking in *Green v. Robinson*,[26] in 1840, Justice Trotter came right to the point:

The [constitutional] convention deemed that the time had arrived, when the traffic in this species of property as "merchandize" should cease. They had seen and deplored the evils connected with it. The barbarities, the frauds, the scenes so shocking in many instances to our feelings of humanity and the sensibilities of our nature, which generally

[25] Dowell v. Boyd, 11 Miss. (3 S. & M.) 592 (1844).
[26] 6 Miss. (5 How.) 80 (1840), holding void as against public policy a contract of sale for slaves imported illegally.

grew out of it, they, therefore, determined to prohibit it in the future. Another alarming evil grew out of it, which was highly dangerous to the moral and orderly condition of our own slaves, and that was the introduction of slaves from abroad of depraved character, which were imposed upon our unsuspecting citizens by the artful and too often unscrupulous negro trader.[27]

In that same case, counsel for appellees had drawn the distinction quite explicitly as he argued in his brief before the high court:

Slavery is one of the favorite institutions of the country; an institution on which rests or depends the wealth, the increasing resources, and the future prospects of the country. Yet I can imagine a man who would hold slaves, who would think it perfectly right to own such property, and cultivate his cotton field by their labor, and yet scorn to make a business of buying and selling human beings for speculation; nay, who would abhor and detest both the speculator and the dealer, and would shun his society. And I can imagine a community of such men. And when I read this clause in the constitution, I see that Mississippi was a community of such.[28]

A second and perhaps more compelling reason for the prohibitory clause was the fear that a swelling slave population might some day wreak vengeance upon its masters. In a strong, cogently argued opinion written in 1846 (where the enforceability of a contract for illegally imported slaves was at issue), Chief Justice Sharkey reviewed the social history of Mississippi up to the year 1832 and stated unequivocally that "a feeling of apprehension began to exhibit itself as early as 1808." [29] Sharkey noted that the constitutional convention of 1817 toyed with the idea of a flat prohibition but finally left the power discretionary with the legislature. Then came other laws authorizing the introduction of slaves only on certain conditions.[30]

Finally, according to the chief justice, the subject occupied

[27] *Ibid.*, 102.   [28] *Ibid.*, 90.
[29] Brien v. Williamson, 8 Miss. (7 How.) 14, 29 (1843).
[30] The chief justice was referring to the act of 1822 prohibiting the importation of convict and African-born slaves.

the serious consideration of the convention of 1832, resulting in the prohibitory clause. "Ultimate public safety was evidently looked to in framing this provision of the constitution. It was equivalent to a declaration of safety." [31]

Having examined the historical background of the prohibitory clause, let us now turn to the controversy it engendered between the two highest courts of state and nation. The first round opened in 1840 when the Mississippi High Court decided two cases arising under this constitutional provision in the same term: *Green* v. *Robinson* [32] and *Glidewell* v. *Hite*. [33] Trouble was immediately apparent.

On the facts, both cases were virtually identical and both reached the court in the same posture. Human nature went its course and slaves were introduced inevitably into the state as merchandise after May 1, 1833, in violation of the constitutional provision, notes being given in the normal course of business as consideration for the slaves. Inevitably, too, the notes were not paid and the holders brought actions at law on them. In neither case was the legal defense raised (which would have been perfectly valid and would have obviated some of the later complications) that, since the contract of sale was illegal, the consideration for the notes was also illegal and the notes therefore unenforceable in a court of law. Instead, the defendant in each case allowed judgment to be entered against him by default, and at that juncture defendant-buyer instituted an equitable action in chancery to enjoin collection of the legal judgments. Two questions were posed: (1) Was the contract void as against public policy? (2) Assuming it to be void, (a) could a court of chancery, after judgment, enjoin execution in order to prevent a void con-

---

[31] Brien v. Williamson, 8 Miss. (7 How.) 14, 30 (1843).
[32] 6 Miss. (5 How.) 80 (1840). Actually *Green* was decided at a former term, but omitted in the reported decisions. The official citation is given here.
[33] 6 Miss. (5 How.) 110 (1840).

tract from being enforced by one of the parties in a court of law? or, (b) must the court of chancery refuse jurisdiction on the technical ground that equity had no power to enjoin against a judgment if a valid defense could have been asserted in a court of law, but was not?

On the first question, both cases held the underlying contract of sale to be void as against public policy, but not without overcoming a vigorous argument by Robinson (the importer-seller) that the simple constitutional provision was not mandatory but merely directory to the legislature, and that until the legislature acted, it had no legal effect ex proprio vigore. Woefully, this argument would later be picked up by the United States Supreme Court. To make matters worse, the legislature did not implement the constitution until 1837, a point in time too late to have any bearing on these cases. However, according to the high court, whether the constitutional clause was mandatory or directory was deemed "immaterial." [34] In either view, it fixed the policy of the state, which the legislature was powerless to counteract.

On the second question, the court held in both cases that it was beyond the power of chancery to relieve the defendants against the judgments for the reason that

Equity, . . . as a general rule, will not interfere where the party could have availed himself of the defence on which he seeks a new trial or injunction, and neglected to make it at the trial.

It is by the observance of this rule that the boundaries between the two jurisdictions can be maintained. The chancellor cannot review the opinions of the law judge, if so the latter might reciprocate reprisals, and a conflict of jurisdiction must ensue, which would be fatal to the steady and regular administration of justice. [35]

Thus, the majority was willing to sacrifice public policy in the interest of keeping the purity of the jurisdictional divide be-

---

[34] Green v. Robinson, 6 Miss. (5 How.) 80, 101 (1840).   [35] *Ibid.*, 105.

tween law and equity. To Justice Sharkey, who was later to
become chief justice, such a doctrine was destructive of the
public policy at stake, and he, for one, would rather sacrifice jurisdictional purity on the altar of public policy:

> That all contracts which are against public policy are absolutely void,
> is a proposition undeniably true. Why I would ask are they so? The an-
> swer is plain; because the public have an interest in the subject matter
> of the contract. The whole community is interested in the suppression
> of vice and immorality, and every thing which tends to disturb the
> peace and harmony, or jeopardize the safety of society. . . . Public
> welfare is paramount to private right, and although each individual may
> take protection under such laws, yet he does so as a member of the
> community, having an interest in common with his fellow citizens in
> having them duly enforced. In cases of this description, public policy is
> in reality the leading object to the adjudication, and it is made exclu-
> sively with a view to guard that policy.[36]

He concluded this point by weighing the respective interests
of society and the private litigants: "The community should not
suffer by the laches of the party to the record. . . . If there is an
interest involved paramount to the interest of the immediate
parties, there can be no reason for an application of the technical
rule of requiring that the defence should have been made at law;
the reason of that rule ceases in a great degree, and so should its
application."[37]

In spite of the cogency of Justice Sharkey's logic, the majority
decision left standing, of course, a judgment "founded on an unconstitutional contract," which the court by enforcing "give[s]
validity to that which was admitted to have none of itself."[38] Already then, a schism had developed on the court as to the net
legal impact of the constitutional provision, and this in turn grew
out of the difference in attitude on the question of the priority of
values as between public policy and the maintenance of a correct

[36] *Ibid.*, 146–47 (dissenting opinion).   [37] *Ibid.*, 147 (dissenting opinion).
[38] Glidewell v. Hite, 6 Miss. (5 How.) 110, 149, 151 (1840) (dissenting opinion of
Sharkey, Ch. J.).

law-equity jurisdiction. At this juncture, *Groves* v. *Slaughter* [39] brought the United States Supreme Court into the dispute and round two was fought out in that tribunal. The facts in *Groves* were fairly typical: Slaughter sued Groves in the federal (circuit) court of Louisiana on a note given for slaves imported as merchandise, for sale, into Mississippi in 1836. Groves, however, promptly raised the defense of the illegality of the consideration at the trial. According to the Supreme Court, "the validity of the defence must turn upon the construction and operation of the . . . article in the constitution of Mississippi adopted on the 26th of October, 1832." [40]

If the Court had wished, it could have dutifully followed the rule of *Elmendorf* v. *Taylor*,[41] which it had enunciated in 1825, that the Supreme Court will adopt that construction of a state statute which has been adopted by the highest court of the state. After all, Chief Justice Sharkey's dissent only reinforced the consensus of the state court that the constitutional provision did in fact declare the public policy of the state and that the contract was void, no matter how the justices might differ over the strength of that policy. Curiously, the Supreme Court rejected the rule of *Elmendorf* at which it nodded in passing, in favor of another maxim which permits the Court to ignore state decisions and interpret the statute for itself where a difference of opinion exists within the state tribunal.[42]

By a review of the *Glidewell* case from its inception in the chancery court of Mississippi, the Court found a sufficient difference of opinion in the state's tribunals to warrant a reopening of the question. After reading the United States Supreme Court's opinion in *Groves*, however, one cannot resist the temptation to say that that Court seemed to relish a battle of words

[39] 40 U.S. (15 Pet.) 449 (1841).   [40] *Ibid.*, 497.
[41] 23 U.S. (10 Wheat.) 152 (1825).
[42] Groves v. Slaughter, 40 U.S. (15 Pet.) 449, 497–98 (1841).

with the Mississippi High Court and chose the course which would gratify that desire. At any rate, from *Groves* v. *Slaughter* came the proposition of law that the vexatious clause in the constitution of 1832 was not mandatory at all, but merely directory, and since the legislature had not spoken, a contract in violation of the constitutional provision could, and would, be enforced.

Four main points were argued by the United States Supreme Court in reaching this decision. First, there were no penalties attached to the constitutional prohibition. Second, the fact that the legislature failed to take action until 1837 suggested that only in 1837 did the provision carry the force of law.[43] Third, the legislative history and opinions of the high court in *Green* and *Glidewell* reflected an unsettled state of opinion surrounding the policy behind the debated clause. Finally, in December, 1833, when the prohibition was purportedly in effect, the legislature passed a law laying a tax on slaves imported as merchandise.[44] This act appeared to the Supreme Court oddly inconsistent with the view that the constitutional clause was operative of its own force.[45] In effect, the legislature had already undermined the position of the state's high court. Chagrined, the Mississippi court waited for an opportunity to salvage the remains of its policy defiled in *Groves*. It came in *Brien* v. *Williamson*,[46] surely the most pontifical word ever written on this particular clause of the constitution.

Given the traditional set of facts—an illegal introduction of slaves and subsequent sale, a promissory note as consideration, a default on the note, and a suit to enforce payment—the high court of Mississippi held once and for all that the contract and note were void and unenforceable, being in violation of the avowed public policy of the state as contained in the now cele-

[43] *Ibid.*, 500–502.
[44] Act of December 23rd, 1833, ch. 10, § 4, *Laws of Mississippi* (Jackson, Miss.: George R. Fall, State Printer, 1834), 49.
[45] Groves v. Slaughter, 40 U.S. (15 Pet.) 449, 501 (1841).
[46] 8 Miss. (7 How.) 14 (1843).

brated clause of the constitution. Not contenting itself with so abbreviated a holding, however, the court responded to the challenge of the United States Supreme Court, point by point. First, of course, it paid homage to the Court itself:

A decision [*Groves* v. *Slaughter*] emanating from a court so justly entitled to our highest respect; one whose decisions are received as authoritative throughout this Union, demands of us that we should review our own decisions, and reconsider the question with the utmost possible scrutiny. This we have endeavored to do, and the result has been to strengthen, if possible, the conviction in the correctness of our former decisions. We regard with great deference the decisions of that exalted tribunal, on questions peculiarly within its province, and in such cases will be always ready to yield to them as authoritative. But state tribunals may justly claim to decide for themselves all questions of state policy, and questions involving the interpretation of state constitutions.[47]

The high court could not resist a passing barb aimed at the lack of unanimity on the Supreme Court itself. Mississippi was still rankling, apparently, under the assault on its own tergiversation:

Still we may well entertain some distrust as to the correctness of our own opinions, when opposed by the decision of the Supreme Court. Our distrust on this occasion is not a little diminished by the reflection that the members of the court were not unanimous in the case of Groves v. Slaughter, and by the additional reflection that amongst the dissenting members there were some who have established for themselves imperishable monuments of judicial fame.[48]

---

[47] *Ibid.*, 16.

[48] *Ibid.* The opinion of Baldwin, J. in Groves v. Slaughter expressed dissatisfaction with those of Justices Thompson, McLean, and Taney. He believed that the contract was valid because the clause in the Mississippi Constitution violated the provision in the United States Constitution giving Congress the power to regulate commerce among the states, and was not a legitimate exercise of the state's police power. "Had the contract in question been invalid by the constitution of Mississippi," he said, "it would be valid by the Constitution of the United States." (*Groves*, at 517.) McLean, J. addressed himself to the same issue of the constitutionality of the clause in the light of the commerce clause, but he concluded that since slaves are treated as persons under the United States Constitution, the commerce clause does not apply to them and the Mississippi Constitution does not, therefore, violate that clause of the United States Constitution (*Groves*, at 506). Taney, C. J. believed the injection of the commerce clause "abstract" (*Groves*, at 510).

Having finished with formalities, the court plunged into the fray. The thrust of the argument was directed, first, at proving the constitutional provision so basic that it required no legislative aid to give it strength:

All fundamental principles, whether inherent or otherwise, in any form of government, constitute a part of the law of that government. When the people prescribe their constitutional form of government, they ordain that every part of that form must have its appropriate effect; every principle is to be regarded as fundamental and self-executing. A constitution need do nothing more than declare first principles.[49]

It then carefully pointed out a familiar distinction between constitutions and codes:

. . . [A] constitution is to be construed as a frame of government, or fundamental law. It is not the business of a convention to deal in detail in all things. From such a body general provisions become fundamental laws. If constitutions were to be construed in all things as mere statutes, many of them would present great ambiguity. But as mere frames these general principles are to have all the force that can be given them to accomplish the object.[50]

The Supreme Court had said as much in *McCulloch* v. *Maryland* back in 1819:

A constitution, to contain an accurate detail of all the subdivisions of which its great powers will admit, and of all the means by which they may be carried into execution, would partake of the prolixity of a legal code, and could scarcely be embraced by the human mind. It would probably never be understood by the public. Its nature, therefore, requires, that only its great outlines should be marked, its important objects designed, and the minor ingredients which compose those objects be deduced from the nature of the objects themselves.[51]

Second, the high court noted the import of the words "shall be" in the constitutional clause was so clearly a prohibition arising from the context of the language that extrinsic aid was inadmissible. Third, since the convention would not have been "insensible" to the fact that a "mere mandate" to the legislature

---

[49] 8 Miss. (7 How.) 14, 18 (1843).   [50] *Ibid.*, 24–25.
[51] 17 U.S. (4 Wheat.) 316, 407 (1819).

might be disregarded, it must have intended "something more than a mandate." Fourth, penalties were not indispensable to accomplish the object of the provision, because the common law punishes for a violation where the legislature fails to provide any specific penalties. Fifth, the court pointed out, the tax law of 1833, which contradicted the prohibition contained in the constitution, was patently unconstitutional and should not have been accorded any weight by the Supreme Court. Sixth, the entire legislative history of the state from 1817 to 1832, and the various acts passed in this period regulating the importation of slaves in the public interest, was evidence of a growing preoccupation of the public mind with this subject. Seventh, in 1832 the legislature submitted to the people an amendment proposing to leave this question with the legislature as a discretionary power, as it stood under the first constitution. The proposition was refused.[52]

"If all this," said the high court, "does not establish the policy of the state, then we must confess that we are wholly at a loss to know what would. Still the supreme court has said that our policy was unsettled." [53] In its final paragraph, the court flung back at the United States Supreme Court one of its own holdings, from *Craig* v. *Missouri*,[54] where no less a figure than John Marshall had asserted that contracts in violation of law or against public policy could not be enforced.

One engagement was over but another was yet to come. Before that issue was joined, however, a period of calm prevailed. The high court of Mississippi contented itself with elaborating on the theme of *Brien* v. *Williamson* and the *Green* and *Glidewell* cases. In a series of decisions beginning in 1845 with *Thomas* v. *Phillips*,[55] it reaffirmed its position and extended the doctrine of those cases to hold void and unenforceable a bond with surety

[52] 8 Miss. (7 How.) at 21, 24, 26–27, 29.   [53] *Ibid.*, 30.
[54] 29 U.S. (4 Pet.) 410, 436 (1830).
[55] 12 Miss. (14 S. & M.) 358 (1845). On the same facts as Glidewell and Green, the court held again that a court of equity will not interfere to give relief against a judgment where the remedy at law was adequate. Again Chief Justice Sharkey dissented.

given subsequent to the original note,[56] a new contract for the endorsement of the original note and an assignment of a mortgage to secure payment,[57] an action by a principal to recover the proceeds of an illegal sale,[58] and a warranty of fitness made in connection with an illegal sale.[59]

In the meanwhile, the constitution was amended in 1844–46 to give the legislature power over the regulation and introduction of slaves into the state.[60] An act was passed in 1846 [61] explicitly repealing the act of 1837, which, it will be remembered, had belatedly caught up with the constitutional prohibition of 1832. What remained on the statute books at this point was an old law of 1822 [62] suddenly given new life by the constitutional amendment of 1846 and the 1846 repealing act. The second stage of the battle was fought over this revived act.

Essentially, the 1822 statute forbade the importation of convict slaves and slaves "born or resident out of the limits of the United States" and required a certificate of good character, to be registered with the orphans' court, for each slave imported. Finally, a penalty of $1,000 was imposed for every convict or African-born slave imported, and $100 fine for any slave bought or sold without a character certificate, the penalty to be imposed on both seller and buyer.[63]

[56] Collins v. McCargo, 14 Miss. (16 S. & M.) 128 (1846).
[57] Adams v. Rowan, 16 Miss. (8 S. & M.) 624 (1847).
[58] Whooten v. Miller, 15 Miss. (7 S. & M.) 380 (1846).
[59] James v. Herring, 20 Miss. (12 S. & M.) 336 (1849).
[60] The act proposing to amend the constitution reads as follows: "The Legislature shall have, and are hereby vested with power to pass such laws regulating or prohibiting the introduction of slaves in this state, as may be deemed proper and expedient." Act of February 24, 1844, ch. 20, § 1, *Laws of Mississippi* (Jackson, Miss.: C. M. Price & S. Rohrer, State Printer, 1844), 133. A Resolution of February 2d, 1846, ch. 288, *Laws of Mississippi* (Jackson, Miss.: C. M. Price & G. R. Fall, State Printers, 1846), 540–41, announced that the above act had received the affirmative vote of a majority of the electors of the state, and pronounced its insertion into the constitution.
[61] Act of February 23, 1846, ch. 63, § 1, *Laws of Mississippi* (Jackson, Miss.: C. M. Price and G. R. Fall, State Printers, 1846), 234.
[62] Act of June 18, 1822, ch. 37, *Hutchinson's Code* (1948), 512.
[63] *Ibid.*, §§ 3–4, 6.

With almost predictable certainty the question was sure to arise whether this act made void and unenforceable on grounds of public policy a note given for the price of non-convict, American-born slaves imported without obtaining a certificate of good character. Indeed the facts were already in the making, and in 1851, without the benefit of a prior state court decision interpreting the act, the Supreme Court of the United States addressed itself to the very question in *Harris* v. *Runnels.*[64] In the light of the earlier controversy over Mississippi's constitutional prohibition against the importation of slaves as merchandise, and in view of its court's impassioned, almost truculent assertion of the policy behind the prohibition in *Brien* v. *Williamson,* the United States Supreme Court was hardly thrown upon its imagination in ascertaining Mississippi's policy as to the effect of an act touching a matter of acute sensitivity to the state. Nor was the Court unmindful of the general rule that contracts made in violation of public policy are void. However, said the Supreme Court, "The rule is certain and plain. The practice under it has been otherwise." [65]

Thereupon, the Court delved into the history of English law on the subject and concluded that "the statute must be examined as a whole, to find out whether or not the makers of it meant that a contract in contravention of it should be void, or that it was not to be so." This meant drawing inferences from the state statute:

When the statute is silent, and contains nothing from which the contrary can be properly inferred, a contract in contravention of it is void.
It is not necessary, however, that the reverse of that should be expressed in terms to exempt a contract from the rule. The exemption may be inferred from those rules of interpretation, to which, from the nature of legislation, all of it is liable when subjected to judicial scrutiny.[66]

[64] 53 U.S. (12 How.) 79 (1851).   [65] *Ibid.*, 83.   [66] *Ibid.*, 84.

Having overcome any procedural inhibitions against subjecting the Mississippi statute to its judicial scrutiny, the Supreme Court proceeded to the dissection. The sufficiency of the penalty provisions suggested to the Court that it was the fine only, without any other loss to either seller or buyer, which was to be inflicted. In addition, since the act was designed primarily to prevent convict Negroes from being imported into the state, and another penalty was provided for that offense, without any provision for forfeiture of the convict, the Supreme Court believed that the legislature would not have intended to deprive the seller of his price for imported slaves who were not convicts, thereby imposing a stiffer penalty on the importer of non-convict slaves than convicts.[67]

Finally, to deny the seller the right to enforce the contract would be to place the defaulting buyer in an advantageous position vis-à-vis the seller. He could keep the slaves and refuse to pay, adding "to his breach of the law the injustice of retaining the Negroes without paying for them." The penalty for violation of the act would, in effect, fall on the seller, the buyer paying his fine from the labor of the slaves. This lack of equality was persuasive to the Court: "Such decided advantages, to one of two who have violated a statute by a contract, could not have been meant by the Legislature of Mississippi." [68]

In its concluding paragraph the Court brushed aside the Mississippi opinions which had so earnestly stated the policy of that state, with a reaffirmation of its own position:

We are aware, that decisions have been made in the courts of Mississippi seemingly in conflict with this; but they are only so in appearance. None of them were made until after the constitution of Mississippi of 1817 had been superseded by that of 1832. We have said, more than once, and now say again, that the clause of the constitution of 1832, prohibiting the introduction of slaves into the State as merchan-

[67] *Ibid.*, 85.   [68] *Ibid.*, 86–87.

dise, was inoperative to prevent it until the legislature acted upon it. We have read all that has been officially written in opposition to that conclusion without having our confidence in its correctness at all shaken.

We shall direct the reversal of the judgment in this case.[69]

Abominable as it was to have one's public policy on a matter of vital interest to the state corrupted again, there was nothing to be done but wait for another case to reach the Mississippi High Court. The familiar facts need not be itemized; they were all present in *Deans* v. *McLendon*,[70] with the result a virtual certainty. This time, however, plaintiff, suing on a defaulted promissory note, did not even get beyond the demurrer stage. After citing the rule that contracts in violation of public policy are void, the high court made a subtle rejoinder to the argument of the inequality of parties made in *Harris* v. *Runnels* without mentioning that case by name:

> Courts of justice, in the observance of these rules, are not influenced by any consideration of respect or tenderness for the party who insists upon the illegality of a contract; but exclusively by reasons of public policy. The object is to punish the active agent in the violation of a law, by withholding from him the anticipated fruits of his illegal act; and thus, by deterring all persons from violating its mandates, to give sanctity to the law and security to the public.[71]

It was only a question of time, however, before the high court got around to disposing of the *Runnels* case politely but firmly. The language of the court speaks for itself:

> It is true, however, that in the case of *Harris* v. *Reynolds* [sic], the Supreme Court of the United States have given a construction to the statute, in direct opposition to that which we consider its proper and legal construction; and have held that the vendor of slaves imported into this state, in violation of the act, is entitled to recover upon a note given for the purchase-money. The question which we have been considering arises upon a statute of this state, designed for the regulation of a subject exclusively within its jurisdiction. We may, therefore, as

---

[69] *Ibid.*   [70] 30 Miss. 343 (1855).   [71] *Ibid.*, 357.

the appellate tribunal of the state, justly claim the right, in exclusion of all other courts, to determine the construction which should be applied to those acts of the legislature passed for the good government of the citizens, and the welfare and safety of the commonwealth; and also to declare and enforce the public policy established by its laws. Hence, however great the respect and deference which may be due to the decisions of the Supreme Court in all cases—and which we willingly pay—we are not bound, and will not yield our well matured and clear convictions, in reference to the construction of our domestic statutes, to the opinions of that tribunal. We could not do so, without grossly betraying the rights of the community, which it is our solemn duty to protect. The Supreme Court, like all other judicial tribunals, in apply-ing the legal rules which grow out of the statutory regulations of any of the states, when they decide in advance, must, of necessity, place their own construction upon them, and determine the validity of those rules. But, in the construction of state statutes, which involve no question arising under the constitution of the United States, or of the laws and treaties made pursuant thereto, it is not the exclusive, nor even the proper expounder. The right to expound, definitely and conclusively, their statutes, and to determine upon what is the public policy, must, of necessity, under our system, belong exclusively to the state courts.

It is not our intention to review the decision in *Harris v. Reynolds* [*sic*], it is sufficient for our purpose to remark, simply, that the reason-ing of the Supreme Court in that case, at best, is unsatisfactory and in-conclusive.[72]

Referring obviously to the earlier conflict over the constitu-tional clause, the court added one more paragraph referring to the "numerous cases" in which "a question completely analo-gous" had been determined by the court which left no doubt as to the outcome of the case in point.[73] So the Mississippi High Court, refusing to give judgment for the price of an illegally im-ported slave, ended in 1855 the litigation over the clause for-bidding the importation of slaves as merchandise.

It was of course quite clear from the beginning what Missis-sippi's policy on this question was, even though the Supreme Court of the United States chose to flout it. In doing so, Missis-sippi policy became the irresistible force meeting an immovable

[72] *Ibid.*, 360–61.   [73] *Ibid.*, 361.

object. No one lost and no one gained anything. Both courts were in a sense right and both were, in another sense, wrong, neither having to capitulate to the other on a matter of state constitutional interpretation. Mississippi was right in that her deep aversion to the importation of slaves as merchandise ran throughout the cases in a gush of emotion mixed with a dose of reason strong enough to permit the inference that a contract in violation of that policy would not be enforced in Mississippi. Certainly by the time of *Harris* v. *Runnels* there was sufficient guidance for the Supreme Court not to wander astray, if it was genuinely trying to ascertain state policy. Mississippi was at fault, however, in initially making herself vulnerable to the Supreme Court on the fine legal point of law-equity jurisdiction, which, together with the legislature's equivocation, gave the Court weaknesses to exploit. On the other hand, the Supreme Court was correct to the extent that the flaws it disclosed were real and significant. Where it erred, however, was in refusing to recognize that technical flaws could not diminish the force of the policy itself, nor the determination of the high court to implement it.[74]

In the end, though, what proved to be more fatal to this policy than either a procedural technicality or the legislature's dilatoriness was the inner contradiction in the social order itself, which the slavetrader first exposed by his obstinate refusal to be stamped out by a mere constitutional prohibition. Not only did he continue to carry on his trade, but he used a formidable body of precedent, holding slaves to be just another "species of property," to derive a plausible claim to the legality of his occupa-

[74] J. F. H. Claiborne has commented on this episode in the court's history as follows: "It will be admitted by every unprejudiced mind, at this day, that the State court was right, and that it was unreasonable to hold that the clause in the constitution, imperative in its terms, and intended to frame the policy of the State, upon a matter of great moment, should be left for its operative effect, to the discretion of the legislature." Claiborne, *Mississippi as a Province, Territory and State*, 476.

tion.[75] His question, simply put, was this: Why deprive the slavetrader alone of his particular benefit from a slaveowning society which allowed all others the right to enjoy an infinite variety of benefits from this institution?

As the high court wrestled with this question, the moral dilemma escaped it completely. Once a society condones and legalizes slavery, it must accept the admittedly evil consequences inherent in its existence along with the economic and social benefits. What the constitution of 1832 and ultimately the high court were attempting, rather, was to draw an untenable distinction between the "good" slaveholders and "bad" slavetraders. The Mississippi court never seemed to recognize the contradiction contained in these two postures which it precariously maintained over the years: (1) that slaveholders are honorable men, and they may deal in slaves in diverse ways as mere chattels; (2) that slavetraders are evil men who engage in a vicious practice which has infected the Mississippi policy and must be eradicated. In fact, the entire episode proves, if nothing else, how difficult, how absurd, how futile it was for a society to try to enforce a public policy suppressing traffic in a commodity which it valued commercially for virtually all purposes.

In the final analysis, it was this inner contradiction which made the defense of the policy against erosion by the United States Supreme Court such a frustrating experience. The Court, by enforcing a contract in obvious violation of the state's constitution and in direct opposition to the state's policy as interpreted by its highest court, said, in effect, that the Mississippi social order belied the avowed purpose behind the prohibition. It thereby exposed the contradiction, and all the forensic might of the high court of Mississippi could not resolve it.

---

[75] It was explicitly argued by counsel in Green v. Robinson, 6 Miss. (5 How.) 80, 103 (1840), that slaves were a species of property recognized as such by the constitution and therefore were the legitimate subject of traffic.

CHAPTER IV

At the Nadir: Manumission

The cases to be analyzed in this chapter plunged the Mississippi High Court for the first time into national political currents where it boldly revealed its constitutional posture vis à vis other states. Again the slavery issue—this time in the form of emancipation [1]—lay at the crux of the matter and shaped the jurisprudence of Mississippi in a singular fashion. Although the highly charged word "emancipation" gave the high court an opportunity to play its role of defender of the faith more brilliantly, more passionately than did any other issue confronting it before the Civil War, that very fire and emotion gave to such cases a quality which seems almost bizarre to a reader of the 1970s.

The action of the drama under consideration here takes place offstage. We hear only the voice of a single towering protagonist (the high court of Mississippi) speaking in crescendo-reaching soliloquies to the forces of darkness (the non-slaveholding states) lurking in the wings where diabolical acts have taken place. A background figure—indeed almost a spectator to the events described, but a valuable support to the high court nonetheless—is

---

[1] The two words "manumission" and "emancipation" are synonymous and will be used interchangeably throughout this chapter.

the Supreme Court of the United States, whose reassuring voice is echoed and remembered rather than directly heard.

Long before what can only be described as paranoia had beset the Mississippi body polity, beginning perhaps in the early 1820s, emancipation was seen as a threat sometimes dimly, sometimes distinctly perceived, but always as a menace necessitating war on four different fronts. At one extreme loomed the fantasy of wholesale emancipation by government decree of some kind from Washington. However, this ultimate dread was too unreal, too remote even to be called a possibility. The specter assumed no tangible form, nor could it be conceived of in any credible historical or political context. And it was certainly not, in the days before the Civil War, the subject matter out of which common cases were made.

At the other extreme were the rare petitions for freedom filed in Mississippi courts by Mississippi slaves or by free Negroes manumitted in other slaveholding states now seeking to enforce recognition of that status in Mississippi. These perturbed the high court scarcely at all, because with the passage of time the cases raising this particular issue became infinitesimal in number,[2] and because this approach to manumission was so entirely controllable by state institutions, i.e., the legislature and the high court.

The problems for the Mississippi High Court arose rather in two broad zones lying between the poles. Decidedly the more irritating of the two (for the reason that it was less amenable to effective control) concerned the practice of non-slaveholding states in, first, freeing fugitive slaves and then, to compound the error, in attempting to confer rights in Mississippi on these

[2] In Sam v. Fore, 20 Miss. (12 S. & M.) 413 (1849), the high court allowed a free Negro emancipated under the laws of Kentucky to establish his right to freedom upon proof of the law of Kentucky; and in Benoit v. Bell, 15 Miss. (7 S. & M.) 32 (1846), it held that petitioner Benoit made a prima facie case of a right to distribution in the estate of his father-slaveholder, upon proof that the state legislature had by act confirmed his manumission.

free Negroes. Less inflammatory but equally repugnant were the actions of those loyal Mississippi slaveholders who tried to emancipate their own slaves by last will and testament. The train of thought behind this contagious vice ran in the mind of the testator something like this: "I have had my enjoyment from slaves, but then, I am the exceptional master. The *idea* of slavery isn't appealing to me anymore, and personally, I should hate to think of anyone else owning my slaves. Therefore, being a magnanimous, benign planter, I hereby will that all my slaves be emancipated upon my death." Multiply this attitude by the number of high-minded slaveowners in Mississippi and the result is an increase in the population of free Negroes in Mississippi, relative to slaves, and a growing social problem. By necessity it became the preoccupation of the state to protect slavery for future generations against the possibility of extinction by self-righteous members of the present. The bulk of the case law wrestled with these two aspects of emancipation simultaneously.

Within this socio-psychological ambiance stood a solid but not quite symmetrical legal edifice which bore down mightily on concrete cases touching the issue. The structure consisted of (1) the United States Constitution and cases arising under the Fugitive Slave Acts of 1793 [3] and 1850,[4] (2) the ancient principles of comity derived from the law of nations, (3) the Mississippi Constitutions of 1817 and 1832, and (4) those statutes of Mississippi designed to eradicate the tumor of emancipation from the body politic.

1. As for the federal Constitution, it seemed clear that the organic law of the land was on the side of Mississippi and the South in the entire sectional struggle, of which foreign eman-

---

[3] Act of February 12, 1793, ch. 7, 1 Stat. 302. This act required the executive authority of any state into which a slave had fled to deliver up the fugitive upon the demand of the executive authority of the state from which he fled.

[4] Act of September 18, 1850, ch. 60, 9 Stat. 462. This act implemented the act of 1793 and spelled out in detail the procedures for its enforcement.

cipation was only one front. Aside from article IV, section 2,[5] and the Supreme Court cases concerning some phase of the rendition of fugitive slaves,[6] *Strader* v. *Graham*[7] held that the question whether certain slaves were freed by going into Ohio with the permission of their master was purely a question of local law over which the Supreme Court had no jurisdiction. The following passage from that opinion was warmly appreciated in Mississippi:

Every State has an undoubted right to determine the *status*, or domestic and social condition, of the persons domiciled within its territory; except insofar as the powers of the States in this respect are restrained, or duties and obligations imposed upon them by the Constitution of the United States. There is nothing in the Constitution of the United States that can in any degree control the law of Kentucky on this subject. And the condition of the negroes, therefore, as to freedom or slavery, after their return, depended altogether upon the laws of that State, and could not be influenced by the laws of Ohio.[8]

Scott v. *Sandford* was to announce in 1858 what Mississippi had known all along: that free persons of the African race could not be citizens of the United States within the meaning of the Constitution of the United States, and accordingly were not entitled to any of the rights, privileges, and immunities guaranteed by that instrument to citizens.[9] That case, it will be recalled, held that the Circuit Court of the United States for the District

---

[5] "A person charged in any State with Treason, Felony, or other Crime, who shall flee from Justice, and be found in another State, shall on Demand of the Executive Authority of the State from which he fled, be delivered up, to be removed to the State having Jurisdiction of the Crime."

[6] Prigg v. Pennsylvania, 41 U.S. (16 Pet.) 539 (1842), giving a slaveowner constitutional authority to seize and recapture runaway slaves in every state of the Union and holding a Pennsylvania statute unconstitutional which punished such recapture; Jones v. Van Zandt, 46 U.S. (5 How.) 215 (1847), reaffirming the constitutionality of the Fugitive Slave Law of 1793 making it a crime to harbor a fugitive slave; Moore v. Illinois, 55 U.S. (15 How.) 13 (1852), upholding the constitutionality of an Illinois statute which punished persons who harbored fugitive slaves or prevented their owners from retrieving them; Ableman v. Booth, 62 U.S. (21 How.) 506 (1858), holding that the Fugitive Slave Act of 1850 was constitutional and that a state court could not by writ of habeas corpus secure release of a prisoner held by federal authorities for violating that act.

[7] 51 U.S. (10 How.) 82 (1850).   [8] *Ibid.*, 93.   [9] 60 U.S. (19 How.) 393 (1858).

of Missouri had no jurisdiction to decide the petition for freedom of Dred Scott, born a slave, who claimed to be free because a former master had taken him to Illinois where slavery could not legally exist.

2. If the United States Constitution and Supreme Court were sources of comfort to Mississippi, comity was a concept which had to be reasoned away, a rule, the breach of which had to be honored by a rationalization. Henry Campbell Black defines comity as "courtesy; respect; a willingness to grant a privilege not as a matter of right but out of deference or good will." [10] In the context of the relations among nations comity is a substitute for a wanting enforceable legal system. Even among the states of the Union, tied together by a Constitution, it was at the time of the events described in this chapter (as it still is) a respected and honorable word. *Bank of Augusta* v. *Earle* [11] held contemporaneously, in 1839, that a Georgia corporation could make a contract in Alabama and sue an Alabama citizen on it there. From that opinion the following admonition of the chief justice later came to haunt the high court of Mississippi:

It has, however, been supposed that the rules of comity between foreign nations do not apply to the states of this Union; that they extend to one another no other rights than those which are given by the Constitution of the United States; and that the Courts of the general government are not at liberty to presume, in the absence of all legislation on the subject, that a state has adopted the comity of nations towards the other states, as part of its jurisprudence; or that it acknowledges any rights but those which are secured by the Constitution of the United States. The Court think otherwise. The intimate union of these states, as members of the same great political family; the deep and vital interests which bind them so closely together, should lead us, in the absence of proof to the contrary, to presume a greater degree of comity, and friendship, and kindness towards one another, than we should be authorized to presume between foreign nations. [12]

[10] *Black's Law Dictionary*, 334 (4th ed., 1951).   [11] 38 U.S. (13 Pet.) 519 (1839).
[12] *Ibid.*, 590.

Many a paragraph was to be devoted in the opinions of the state high court to overcoming the eloquent persuasiveness of Chief Justice Taney's language. If it could not in good conscience heed his advice and accord Negroes freed by abolitionist states rights in Mississippi, at least the high court felt the pressure of comity strongly enough to warrant an explanation for its nonobservance. As for the Negro involved in the particular case, it was a sad story of an individual caught between conflicting philosophies on the institution of slavery, and he was usually the immediate loser.

3. In both Mississippi Constitutions of 1817 and 1832 appeared a single unnumbered article embracing every point on the subject of slavery deemed necessary to be put into a constitution. It was entitled simply "Slaves" and it began:

> The legislature shall have no power to pass laws for the emancipation of slaves, without the consent of their owners, unless where a slave shall have rendered to the state some distinguished service, in which case the owner shall be paid a full equivalent of the slave so emancipated. . . . They [the legislature] shall have power to pass laws to permit the owners of slaves to emancipate them, saving the rights of creditors, and preventing them from becoming a public charge.

What happened to these constitutional clauses leads us to the last prop supporting the legal structure; namely, the Mississippi statutes. Essentially the first constitutional clause (emancipation without the owner's consent) was ignored by the legislature, but the idea of requiring a special legislative act to free a slave was incorporated into law when the legislature implemented the second constitutional provision, relating to emancipation by the owner. As time went on, the general assembly read the second provision to mean that it also had the authority to pass laws forbidding owners from emancipating their slaves. The clause became in effect the grant of a negative power.

4. Actually, only two basic acts constituted the entire statu-

tory scheme regulating emancipation in Mississippi from 1822, to the end in 1863—the acts of 1822 [13] and 1842. [14] Before 1822 there *was* no law on the subject. It was the halcyon period when emancipation was not a dread but simply a transitional stage between slavery and freedom. *Harry* v. *Decker*, the first case reported in the Mississippi Reports, belongs to this tranquil age. We shall return to it momentarily for a closer analysis.

Although it was an omnibus piece of legislation on the subject of slavery, the act of 1822 contained but two sections meriting consideration here. Section 76 spelled out the procedure by which "any person . . . who shall conceive himself or herself illegally detained as a slave in the possession of another" could, after first posting bond, "petition to the circuit court of the county, where his or her master or owner shall reside" for a jury trial on the issue. This procedure—the *only* procedure by which a putative slave could claim his freedom [15]—survived throughout the entire antebellum era. It appeared verbatim in all the codes published between 1822 and 1860. [16]

Section 75 of the same act implemented the constitutional clause giving the legislature power to permit owners to emancipate their slaves. That section first limited a master's right to emancipate to the particular form of a "last will or testament" or "other instrument in writing," under seal. Second, it required the owner to "prove to the satisfaction of the General Assembly, that such slave or slaves have done or performed some meri-

[13] Act of June 18, 1822, § 75, *Laws of Mississippi* (n.p., P. Ister, State Printer, n.d.), 198.

[14] Act of February 26, 1842, ch. 4, § 11, *Laws of Mississippi* (Jackson, Miss.: C. M. Price and G. R. Fall, State Printers, 1842), 69–70.

[15] In Thornton v. Demoss, 13 Miss. (5 S. & M.) 609 (1856), Chief Justice Sharkey underscored the exclusivity of the remedy by saying that "color is *prima facie* evidence of liability to servitude. It is *prima facie* evidence of property in someone, and as a specific remedy is provided for removing the presumption, that remedy necessarily excludes every other and must be strictly pursued."

[16] Ch. 11, § 48 *Howard and Hutchinson's Digest* (1840), 166; ch. 37, art. 2, § 76 *Hutchinson's Code* (1848), 523; ch. 33, § 3, art. 10 *Revised Code* (1857), 236–37.

torious act for the benefit of such owner or owners, or some distinguished service for the benefit of this state." Finally, it declared that the will or other instrument should have no validity
until sanctioned by an act of the general assembly, and until the
owner complied with all the conditions specified in the special
act. Thus, already in 1822, the legislature reserved for itself the
final decision on the emancipation of any slave, even while permitting owners the right to initiate the process.

By 1842 this posture of controlled permissiveness changed to
one of unmitigated hardness. The statute enacted in that year
made it "unlawful for any person, by last will or testament, to
make any devise or bequest of any slave or slaves for the purpose of emancipation, or to direct that any slave or slaves shall
be removed from this state *for the purpose of emancipation elsewhere.*" (Emphasis added.) For such an "unlawful" act a testator
suffered the penalty of having his bequest of freedom thwarted.
The slaves so honored were to "descend to, and be distributed
amongst the heirs at law of the testator, or be otherwise disposed of according to law in the same manner as if such testator
had died intestate." [17]

Basically the same statute was reenacted in the Revised Code
of 1857 in a more stringent form, aimed at preventing secret
trusts for the purpose of emancipation and prohibiting any "colonization society" from taking slaves as grantee under a will. [18]

Whether the act of 1842 entirely achieved its purpose is prob-
lematical, but it precipitated a tangle of litigation involving (a)
the meaning of the phrase "emancipation elsewhere," (b) the
role of the American Colonization Society, and (c) the penalty
provision. Out of its twisted strands the court struggled until the
coming of the Civil War to pull a single continuing thread of
thought. One final piece of legislation must be mentioned to

[17] Act of February 26, 1842, ch. 4, § 11, *Laws of Mississippi* (Jackson, Miss.: C. M.
Price and G. R. Fall, State Printers, 1842), 70.
[18] Ch. 33, § 3, art. 9 *Revised Code* (1857), 236.

complete the legal structure. This measure, originally section 50 of the omnibus act of 1822, rounded out to perfection the statutory scheme by prohibiting free Negroes and mulattoes from immigrating to and residing in Mississippi. Failure to leave the state after thirty days' notice resulted in arrest, incarceration, and eventually the auction block. Those few free Negroes permitted to reside in the state by special legislative dispensation were severely restricted in their movements and had to carry certificates of freedom at all times in order to avoid jailing. All three of the Mississippi Codes extant before the Civil War contained the substance if not the precise language of section 50.[19] As might be expected, the act of 1842 stiffened the language of section 50 and added an extra penalty of thirty-nine lashes to be meted out to a free Negro who was unwilling to leave the state before being sold into slavery.[20]

Given the issue as it was framed in the two specific formulations mentioned earlier in this chapter—(1) the right of Mississippi testators to emancipate their slaves, and (2) the rights in Mississippi of Negroes emancipated by non-slaveholding states—it became the function of the high court not simply to articulate and interpret a public policy embraced in a particular cluster of statutes, but on a far more ambitious scale to define the image and fashion the unique identity of Mississippi, past, present, and future. Actually, the high court grew into this role. The emotional fervor, the clarity of its vision as defender of the faith, the savagery and moral indignation of the opinions, none of these happened overnight. They came as the court engaged in mortal combat with forces bent on destroying the state's most precious resource.

The prelude to the court's output is the singular case of *Harry*

[19] Ch. 11, §§ 50–53, *Howard and Hutchinson's Digest* (1840), 167–69; ch. 37, art. 2, §§ 80–86, *Hutchinson's Code* (1848), 524–25; art. 10, § 1, *ibid.*, 533; ch. 33, § 12, art. 79–81, *Revised Code* (1857), 253.

[20] Act of February 26, 1842, ch. 4, § 3, *Laws of Mississippi* (Jackson, Miss.: C. M. Price and G. R. Fall, State Printers, 1842), 70.

v. *Decker*, decided in 1818. Its singularity lies primarily in the
tone and style of the opinion, however, rather than in the holding (which was no small point of law in itself). The court ruled
that three Negroes, who had been slaves in Virginia prior to the
Treaty of Cession of 1763 but who later moved to the Northwest
Territory with their master, were freed by the Northwest Ordinance of 1787 and were entitled to assert that freedom in Mississippi. The following lines from the opinion, written by an anonymous justice of the high court, deserve quoting because they
typify the spirit of liberty which pervaded the case as a whole:

> Slavery is condemned by reason and the laws of nature. It exists and
> can only exist, through municipal regulations, and in matters of doubt,
> is it not an unquestioned rule that courts must lean "in favorem vitae et
> libertatis." Admitting it was a doubtful point, whether the constitution
> was to be considered prospective in its operation or not, the defendants
> say, you take from us a vested right arising from municipal law. The
> petitioners say you would deprive us of a natural right guaranteed by
> the ordinance and constitution. How should the Court decide, if con-
> struction were really to determine it? I presume it would be in favour
> of liberty.[21]

That case could have no sequel. The moral philosophy expressed
in the opinion on the institution of slavery was only a romantic
historical error of 1818, antagonistic to the forces at work in the
state which were eventually to venerate slavery as one of the
noblest inventions of man and consign *Harry* to oblivion.

Let us now watch the action of the court in the line of cases
touching the problem of attempted manumission in wills executed by Mississippi testators. In *Ross* v. *Vertner*,[22] a case
predating the act of 1842, one Captain Isaac Ross directed in his
will that his executors should send his slaves to Liberia "there to
be settled and remain free." Neither he nor the executors made
any attempt to comply with the 1822 law, which required a
special legislative act on proof of meritorious service by the

---

[21] 1 Miss. (Walk.) 36, 42–43 (1818).   [22] 6 Miss. (5 How.) 305, 357 (1840).

slave. Under these circumstances the issue was joined whether the will raised a valid trust, and oddly enough the court held that it did, in spite of the precedent set by *Hinds* v. *Brazealle* [23] decided just the year before, and which was distinguished on the facts. To Justice Trotter, writing the opinion in *Ross*, the act of transporting the slaves to Liberia "there to remain free" did not seem to be an act of manumission within the meaning of the statute in its spirit of policy. He reasoned:

Placed thus beyond our limits, their freedom could not be the subject of animadversion by the municipal laws of Mississippi, whose rigorous police regulations on this subject, were designed for the security of slave owners in the state, against the dangers of too great an increase of free negroes, whose example and whose means too of sowing the seeds of mischief, of insubordination, perhaps of revolt, amongst the slaves in their neighborhood, was very justly to be apprehended and guarded. It is not the policy of Mississippi to augment her slave population. In her written constitution she has spoken her will in unequivocal language, and the fiat there made of her future policy has been seconded by the sternest legislative sanctions. [24]

The last two sentences of that quotation are significant. Justice Trotter was saying, in effect, that the policy of the state was not against manumission ipso facto, but only against the increase of the Negro population in Mississippi. The constitutional clause prohibiting the introduction of slaves as merchandise, the implementing act of 1837, and a liberal reading of the act of 1822 were all evidence to the justice of the correctness of his position. History was to prove him wrong, but before the last words were written on this subject, *Ross* spawned a group of cases emulating its "soft" approach to emancipation.

In *Shattuck* v. *Young* [25] the high court gave a sympathetic interpretation to a will directing the executor to represent to the legislature the meritorious services of a Negro slave, and to

<hr>

[23] 3 Miss. (2 How.) 837 (1838).   [24] 6 Miss. (5 How.) at 360.
[25] 10 Miss. (2 S. & M.) 30, 36 (1844).

procure from the legislature an act for his emancipation. No less a figure than Chief Justice Sharkey reasoned that this clause did not propose to emancipate, but only laid the foundation for a legal emancipation. But further on in the opinion is noted the sad ending to *Shattuck* v. *Young;* the legislature refused to cooperate, and the slaves accordingly had to fall into the residue of the estate.

On facts almost identical to those in *Ross*, the court upheld a will in *Leech* v. *Cooley*, [26] in which a certain Mr. Leech directed that four of his slaves "be set free, and sent to Indiana or Liberia as they may prefer." Citing the *Ross* case, Justice Clayton observed that the order of the words was inverted. Here the slaves were to be set free and *then* sent off, while in the *Ross* case they were to be sent first to Liberia, *there* to be freed. However, he reasoned that "the mere collocation of words" could not alter their construction. Then, adopting the *Ross* rationale he continued:

It is the policy of this state, as evinced by its legislation, to prevent the increase of free persons of color therein. No one is permitted to emancipate a slave by deed or by will, to remain in the state without the consent of the legislature, specially obtained. If a free person of color come from another state into this, and remain beyond a certain time, he may be apprehended and sold. Nor is this legislative policy controlled by the provision in the constitution of the United States, which declares, "that the citizens of each state shall be entitled to all privileges and immunities of citizens in the several states." No person of color can become a citizen in this sense of the term. They may become denizens in particular states, and may enjoy in them all the rights of citizenship, so far as state legislation can confer those rights. But when they leave the limits of such state, and enter another, they become subject to the laws of the latter, and must be governed by them. The general government does not interfere with the regulations of the states in this respect. [27]

Obviously no justice or court in Mississippi, whether soft or hard in the approach to emancipation, could contemplate the

[26] 14 Miss. (6 S. & M.) 93 (1846).   [27] *Ibid.*, 98–99.

Negro as a citizen. In this respect Mississippi was entirely within
the purview of what was to become the doctrine of *Dred Scott*.
But that truth, according to *Leech*, did not prevent the emancipation of the slaves in Indiana or Liberia. The court went on to
say that it saw "nothing in the law" to prevent it. "The right to
freedom under the will is inchoate, and becomes complete,
when the subjects of it are removed to another state or country." [28] Perhaps the strangest aspect of the case, however, was
its utter lack of concern about or apparent knowledge of the
stern act of 1842. Not one word of the court's opinion was devoted to it—a striking oversight in the light of the policy expressed in that act. In short, *Leech* v. *Cooley* carried the "soft"
approach considerably further than its predecessor, and the incredible omission rendered the case extremely vulnerable to
later criticism.

The contest in *Wade* v. *American Colonization Society* [29]
grew out of the same will which was the subject of the controversy in *Ross* v. *Vertner*. In that case, it will be recalled, the
action was brought by the heirs and distributees of the testator,
against the executors, to prevent the execution of the trusts of
the will; in the present case the American Colonization Society,
as trustee, brought the action against the executors, six years
after the decision in *Ross*, to compel the execution of these
trusts and to carry out the provisions of the will. Overcoming
the argument that the American Colonization Society had no capacity to take because its charter was inconsistent with the
bequests in the will, the Mississippi High Court argued as follows:

It is again insisted that this society is prohibited by its character from
taking or holding property except for one purpose, that "of colonizing
with their own consent upon the coast of Africa, the free people of
color residing in the United States." We do not give to the charter the
same restricted construction that the counsel do. It is true the charter

28 *Ibid.*, 99.   29 15 Miss. (7 S. & M.) 663 (1846).

confers no right to transport *slaves* to Africa. But the slaves of to-day may be free tomorrow, and when free, may with their own consent be so transported. In the present instance these slaves are not now free, but they have an inchoate right to freedom. As soon as they are taken beyond the limits of this state, that right is so far consummated, that by the terms of the charter they may be transported and colonized. In this there is no violation either of the laws of the state or of the charter; and such provisions have been repeatedly carried into effect by the society without objection.[30]

The effect of the decision was simply to compel the execution of the trusts, but the court concluded its opinion with a sound rebuke to the executors for their dilatoriness. One cannot help wonder whether the slaves ever made it to Africa.

In diametrical opposition to these sympathetic cases, a parallel "hard" line which eventually became the "correct" doctrine of the state, began with *Luckey* v. *Dykes*,[31] decided one year after the act of 1842. Unlike *Leech*, however, which was also decided after this significant legislation, *Luckey* v. *Dykes* felt its presence and power. Without direct citation, the court held that the last will and testament of a William Johnson, who directed that his slaves be emancipated upon his death, was void because "in opposition to our state policy." What troubled the court was the second question raised concerning the disposition of the slaves. In the light of the penalty clause of the act of 1842, providing that such slaves should pass to the heirs at law as if the testator had died intestate, were they to go to the next of kin, or to the residuary legatees under the will? After some labor, the court held for the next of kin on the ground that there was no true residuary clause in the will.[32]

---

[30] *Ibid.*, 697.   [31] 10 Miss. (2 S. & M.) 60, 68 (1843).

[32] Incidentally, this penalty provision in the 1842 law created litigation in future cases between heirs at law, claiming under the 1842 act, and residuary legatees claiming under a rule of the common law that the general residuary legatee takes whatever by lapse or invalid disposition falls into the residue of the estate. Regrettably, the court was not entirely consistent in this sub-area of the law of emancipation either. Read v. Manning, 30 Miss. 308 (1855), held that a bequest of freedom in a codicil to a will was absolutely void

That all Mississippi testators fell under the ban of the act of 1842 was indisputable; but whether the prohibition applied to a domiciliary of another state who owned slaves in Mississippi and attempted to emancipate them by a will executed there the statute left unanswered. This was the problem posed by *Mahorner* v. *Hooe*.[33] The case is a critical one for two reasons: (1) It measured better than any of the "domestic" manumission cases the degree to which the court had moved on this issue by 1848 (the date of *Mahorner*); and (2) it came to grips with three sub-issues which converged within it—comity, the act of 1842, and the constitutional clause forbidding the importation of slaves as merchandise. In holding that a Virginia testator, who emancipated all his Mississippi slaves by will with instructions that they be sent to Africa, had violated the public policy of Mississippi and so died intestate with respect to the slaves in Mississippi, the court allied itself with the hard school. To disproving the argument that comity required the application of the laws of Virginia, where the bequest was valid, the court devoted five full pages, yielding with the right hand and denying with the left: "And whilst we freely concede that in this confederacy of states, comity is indispensable, and should be extended in the most ample manner, yet it cannot be allowed to defeat the general policy of a state, declared by legislative authority."[34]

Moreover, the high court found the public policy of the state to be unequivocally expressed in the act of 1842, which could be easily reconciled with the constitutional provision prohibiting the introduction of slaves as merchandise:

---

and the slaves were subject to distribution; Cheairs v. Smith, 37 Miss. 646 (1859), held that a provision in a will for the emancipation of slaves did not avoid the whole will as to distinct and independent provisions, not connected with the illegal purpose; the will was void only as to the slaves attempted to be emancipated. Garnett v. Cowles, 39 Miss. 60 (1860), held that if the primary intent of the testator was that his slaves should be emancipated, he could make a secondary alternative disposition of them, giving the slaves to his residuary legatee. The residuary legatee prevailed over the heirs.

[33] 17 Miss. (9 S. & M.) 247 (1848).   [34] *Ibid.*, 278.

And here we would say a word in reference to an objection made to this law on the ground of its being contrary to the policy of that provision in the constitution which, at the time, prohibited the introduction of slaves into this state. We do not perceive any such repugnancy as would avoid the law. It might have been good policy to exclude slaves (that provision has been changed); and it may also be good policy to retain what we have. At all events it was competent to discountenance emancipation by last will and testament, by defeating the declared intention of the testator, although that intention was to be consummated beyond the limits of the state. A sovereignty may guard its policy by imposing restrictions on all property within its limits. It may look to the ultimate destination of that property abroad; and if that destination be incompatible with the best interests of the state, the intention of the testator may be defeated if it has been made known. We accordingly think the law of 1842 is a valid prohibition, paramount to that rule of comity, which, in the absence of such prohibition, might sustain the bequest on the law of the testator's domicil.[35]

Lusk v. *Lewis,*[36] decided in 1856, was the "hard" counterweight to *Wade* v. *American Colonization Society* of some ten years earlier. It held void a bequest of slaves "in trust for the American Colonization Society," but now the court penetrated into the real nature of that entity. It was the character of the society as basically antagonistic to slavery which invalidated the trust and formed the basis of the court's rationale:

. . . [T]he establishment of the society had a tendency to encourage emancipation, if indeed that was not an object within the especial contemplation of the institution. Its operation was calculated strongly to promote emancipation, and it may, therefore, be regarded as founded on a principle not consistent with the growth and permanency of the institution of slavery; for it cannot be supposed that an effect so obvious was not intended as a part of the system.
. . . And, considering the policy and objects of the institution, we think that the society must be regarded as having no further title or interest in them [the slaves] than for the purpose of emancipation and colonization, and that the bequests of the will were made for that purpose. This comes within the prohibition of our Statute of 1842, and the bequests must, therefore, be declared illegal and void.[37]

[35] *Ibid.*   [36] 32 Miss. 297 (1856).   [37] *Ibid.*, 301–302.

Thus, although a split had developed in the high court on the question of whether the act of 1842 or the constitutional clause prohibiting the importation of slaves as merchandise embodied the true policy of the state, the opinions discussing the issue were still moderate in tone and decidedly rational in analysis. A similar division quickly arose over the question whether Negroes emancipated elsewhere could enjoy rights in Mississippi. With the passing of years, however, and the approach of the Civil War, rational analysis gave way to irrational invective, and moderation to passion.

As early as 1838, *Hinds* v. *Brazealle* had refused to give effect to a deed of emancipation executed by a Mississippi slaveholder in Ohio. Elisha Brazealle had taken with him to that state a Negro woman and her son John for the express purpose of emancipation. Having accomplished his purpose in Ohio, the threesome returned to Mississippi where they lived until Brazealle's death. In his will he acknowledged John to be his son and devised his entire estate to him. The heirs at law claimed the deed of emancipation was void.

In deciding for the heirs, the court dismissed rules of comity summarily:

> Upon principles of national comity, contracts are to be construed according to the laws of the country or state where they are made, and the respective rights and duties of the parties are to be defined accordingly. As these laws derive their force entirely from comity, they are not to be adopted to the exclusion of state laws by which the great and fundamental policy of the state is fixed and regulated. And hence it follows that this rule is subject to exceptions. No state is bound to recognize or enforce a contract made elsewhere, which would injure the state or its citizens; or which would exhibit to the citizens an example pernicious and detestable.[38]

Thus, not only did John fail to take by devise the estate of his former master-father, but the court held he was still a slave and

[38] 3 Miss. (2 How.) 837, 842 (1838).

passed accordingly as property under the will. But twenty-five years later, in *Leiper* v. *Hoffman*,[39] the court took a different tack. Petitioner was a former Mississippi slave. In 1834 her master had set her free, but he neglected to apply to the legislature for its sanction. Technically a slave, then, she purchased in 1834 real property in Mississippi and resided on it until 1845, when she left for Ohio with her "master." Petitioner had the deed to her property put in her name jointly with defendant W., a white person. During her years of residence in Ohio the property came by fraud into the ownership and possession of defendant *H*. Petitioner sought in this action a cancellation of the deed to *H*. and surrender of possession to her. Distinguishing *Hinds* v. *Brazealle* on the factual difference that her change of residence to Ohio was *bona fide* rather than a stratagem to evade the law of Mississippi, and completely ignoring the "hard" line of cases which had gone before, while citing *Ross* v. *Vertner*, the court granted petitioner all the relief sought. No more agreeable view of petitioner's position could be dreamt of than actually appeared in the following paragraph from the court's opinion:

. . . It is contended that the complainant took nothing by the deed to her and Winscott, because she was a slave at the date of it. It is not necessary to decide what would have been the effect of the deed, if it had been made in her name alone, she being a slave, but her legal owner treating her as free, and her freedom having been subsequently established. If the deed was inoperative to convey any legal or equitable estate *in presenti*, it was still effectual as a conveyance of the legal title to Winscott. And it was competent for him to hold the legal title in trust for her. Her right of present enjoyment might be prevented by her condition of slavery; but if the trust continued until that disability was removed by her admission to the rights of a free person, her rights as a *cestui que trust* would then immediately vest, and she would be entitled to enforce them against the trustee. While she was still a slave, her rights were suspended, and no one could interfere with them but her legal owner. Here that person fully acquiesces in her claim both

---

[39] 26 Miss. 615 (1853).

before and since the establishment of her freedom, and no other person can question her rights acquired under the deed. She is, therefore, entitled to claim the benefit of the trust; and if the trustee has aliened the trust property, it is chargeable in the hands of any one into whose possession it has come, with legal notice of her claim.[40]

Shaw v. *Brown*, coming in 1858, marked the outer limits of the policy of tolerance. In holding that a free Negro from Indiana could take a pecuniary bequest under a will executed in Mississippi by a Mississippi testator, the court, citing *Dred Scott*, considered the status of free Negroes in general:

But Negroes born in the United States, and free by the laws of the State in which they reside, are in a different condition from aliens. They are natives, and not aliens. Though not *citizens* of the State in which they reside, within the meaning of the Constitution of the United States, they are *inhabitants* and *subjects* of the State, owing allegiance to it, and entitled to protection by its laws and those of the United States; for by the common law, and the law of nations, all persons born within the dominion of the sovereign are his natural born subjects, and owe allegiance to him, and obedience to the laws, and are entitled to protection.[41]

Reasoning from principles of international law and comity, the court considered the Negro's status equivalent to that of an alien whose domestic rights would be respected in foreign tribunals: "Hence the rights of persons, as they are fixed by the law of their domicil, are observed and enforced in the tribunals of foreign civilized nations, unless they are prejudicial to the rights or powers of those governments, or in contravention of their public policy, or positive law." [42]

Weaving comity in with the Constitution, the court continued:

Accordingly, the doctrine is sanctioned by the Supreme Court of the United States, that these principles of international law apply with greater force between the people of the several States, than as between the subjects of foreign nations. *Bank of Augusta v. Earle.* In that case,

[40] 26 Miss. at 622.   [41] *Ibid.*, 315.   [42] *Ibid.*, 316.

the court disapproved of the doctrine, "that the States extend to each other no other rights than those which are given by the Constitution of the United States;" and held that a bank incorporated by one State might acquire rights in another State, and enforce them by suit.[43]

The court then asked: "Is it, then, against the policy of our laws that free negroes of other States of the Union should be capable of having any rights whatever in this State? We think not." [44]

Since the pecuniary bequest would not entail the presence of the freed slave in Mississippi, and he would therefore have no personal intercourse with Mississippi slaves, the court capsulized its rationale by stating:

The *status* of freedom in the negro, may be considered as discountenanced here in principle, because not in consonance with our practice. But that has no practical effect upon his *status* elsewhere; and it could not be justly considered as an inhibition of his rights, legally acquired under the laws of his domicil, and which might be exercised here, without subjecting our slaves to the mischief, intended to be prevented by our laws, arising from the presence of free negroes here, and their influence upon our slaves.[45]

Relying, then, upon principles of the Constitution as well as international law, and finding the policy of Mississippi compatible with the idea of manumission outside the state, these cases evolved a remarkably lenient body of law governing the rights of foreign-emancipated slaves in Mississippi. The whole structure was to come tumbling down, however, with the case of *Heirn* v. *Bridault* [46] decided just one year after *Shaw* v. *Brown*. Far surpassing *Hinds* v. *Brazealle* in posture and *Dred Scott* in tone, the opinion is the work of a court obsessed. The holding was no more than that a "free woman of color" from Louisiana was incapable of taking property by devise in Mississippi, but the dicta referred to Negroes as *"alien strangers*, of an inferior class, incapable of comity, with whom our government has no commer-

[43] *Ibid.*, 317.   [44] *Ibid.*, 318.   [45] *Ibid.*, 319.   [46] 37 Miss. 209 (1859).

cial, social or diplomatic intercourse." Furthermore, said the court:

> . . . [T]he law of nations, having its origin in the necessities growing out of commercial, social, and diplomatic intercourse of civilized nations, and being bounded upon the express or implied assent of such nations, cannot be extended to embrace those nations or people who neither respect nor acknowledge the laws of God or man, and are wholly incapable, from their nature and constitution, of *civilized* intercourse. "The law of nations is a system of rules, which reason, morality, and custom have established among *civilized* nations as their public law." [47]

In conclusion the high court did not hedge on what it believed the policy of Mississippi to be:

> It is, therefore, the policy of this State to interdict all intercourse, commerce, and comity with this race; and by law, expressly provided, we enforce the strictest doctrines of the ancient law, as applicable to *alien enemies*, except as to life or limb, against them. We enslave them for life, if they dare set their foot on our soil, and omit to leave on notice in ten days. And this not upon the principle, supposed by some, of enmity, inhumanity, or unkindness, to such inferior race, but on the great principles of self-preservation, which have induced civilized nations in every age of the world to regard them as only fit for slaves, as wholly incapable, morally and mentally, of appreciating or practising, without enlightenment, the principles and precepts of the Divine and natural law, upon which the laws of international comity are founded.[48]

In truth, there was not much left for *Mitchell* v. *Wells*, in 1859, to do after that. There a "free woman of color," a domiciliary of Ohio and the alleged daughter of testator Wells was held incapable of taking property bequeathed her under a Mississippi will by a Mississippi resident. The chief contribution of this case lay in its collating and reviewing all the decisions in this area and then establishing in bold, decisive language precisely what the policy of the state would be henceforth. "I hold," said Justice Harris, writing the opinion of the court:

[47] *Ibid.*, 230.   [48] *Ibid.*, 232.

1st. That comity is subordinate to sovereignty, and cannot, therefore, contravene our public policy, or the rights, interests, or safety of our State or people.

2d. That the emancipation, either here or elsewhere, of slaves domiciled in this State, is against our policy, institutions, and laws.

3d. That all laws of other States, and all acts of their citizens or ours, in opposition to our public policy, are void *within the limits of Mississippi*, whatever validity they may be allowed elsewhere.

4th. That the status of a slave, in Mississippi is fixed by our laws, and cannot be changed elsewhere, so as to give him a *new status in this State*, without our consent.

5th. That a slave can neither acquire freedom, nor a new domicile, nor any other right or capacity in another state, to be enjoyed in Mississippi, in violation of our policy.

6th. That neither the right to sue, nor the right to acquire or hold property in this State, nor the right to any privileges belonging to free white citizens, or inhabitants of other States or nations, accorded by comity, can be conferred upon the African race, in the State of Mississippi, by the authority of another State or nation.[49]

The 1859 *Mitchell* case was the last word ever spoken by the Mississippi High Court on this issue before the Civil War, and it was coupled with an indictment against the state which in this case had precipitated the problem:

The State of Ohio, forgetful of her constitutional obligations to the whole race, and afflicted with a *negro-mania*, which inclines her to *descend*, rather than elevate herself in the scale of humanity, chooses to take to her embrace, as citizens, the neglected race, who by common consent of the States united, were regarded, at the formation of our government, as an inferior caste, incapable of the blessings of free government, and occupying, in the order of nature, an intermediate state between the irrational animal and the white man.

In violation of good faith, as well as of the guarantees of the Constitution, efforts are made to destroy the rights of property in this race, which, at the time of the adoption of that instrument, was in servitude, in all or nearly all the States originally parties to the compact of Union. Mississippi and other States, under the firm conviction, that the relation of master and slave, which has existed within her limits, from the organization of the State government to this day, is mutually produc-

[49] 37 Miss. 235, 249 (1859).

tive of the happiness and best interests of both, continues the institution, and desires to perpetuate it. She is unwilling to extend to the slave race freedom and equality of rights, or to elevate them into political association with the family of States.[50]

That the emotion surrounding the slavery question had indeed infiltrated the high court is dramatized by the following passage from the dissenting opinion of Justice Handy in *Mitchell:*

It is said that the violation by the non-slaveholding States, of the constitutional rights of the Southern States, in harboring our fugitive slaves and in furnishing them protection against the claims of their owners, deprives them of all claim to international comity in reference to the rights of their free negroes who may seek to assert rights in our courts.

But this sacred duty,—to respect and enforce the rights of residents of other States, secured to them by the laws of those States,—can never be destroyed, whilst the confederacy continues, by the fact that the State under which the right is claimed, has been recreant to her obligations to the compact which binds the States together. If their courts of justice have been prostituted to the purposes of fanaticism and lawlessness, that is no reason why we should descend from our elevated position, which should be superior to such influences, follow their unworthy example, and make this court the medium of propagating our political theories upon the same subject. Whilst the confederacy continues, we cannot justify ourselves as a State in violating its spirit and principles, because other States have, in some respects been false to their duties and obligations. It may justify us in dissolving the compact, but not in violating our obligations under it whilst it continues.[51]

The Civil War could not be far off.

CONCLUSIONS

The schizophrenia within the high court, which only mirrored the deeper one existing in the state as a whole, resulted in two conflicting lines of cases on the issue of manumission: one, holding the policy of the state to be merely against the increase of free Negroes in Mississippi, but not against their manumission

[50] *Ibid.,* 262–63.   [51] *Ibid.,* 285.

elsewhere; and the other, opposed to emancipation in any form, anywhere. A similar dichotomy developed over the issue of permitting slaves emancipated in abolitionist states to take property in Mississippi. As the court teetered back and forth between these conflicting positions, the division between the cases became increasingly pronounced until in 1859 the court in *Mitchell* v. *Wells* had to admit: "Reconciliation would seem impossible; they are directly in conflict, and upon questions of vital importance." [52] That case simply solved the problem by castigating the "weak" and embracing as the true state policy the stance of the "hard" cases, while carrying the rationale to a much more extreme position. Together with the foreshadowing case of *Heirn* v. *Bridault, Mitchell* marked the zenith of the court's career as defender of the faith and the nadir of its descent from tempered political objectivity. These two cases epitomize the moral outrage, the fanaticism, and righteous fury which pervaded the state as a whole as the Civil War came closer. By 1859 the high court was in truth engaged in a battle between what it perceived as the forces of good and evil.

In this sensitive area of manumission, the legal issues became confused with the bitter political struggle separating the slaveholding from the abolitionist states. As the court became more rabid on the subject of emancipation, it sought a legal theory as extreme, distorted and irrational as its emotional attitude. The legal theory that free Negroes were "enemy aliens" simply followed the psychological pitch of the high court. It could view with alarm tinged with a measure of understanding attempts by Mississippians to emancipate their slaves by will and send them out of state; but it could not view the slightest act of an abolitionist state tending to impinge on its sacred institution with anything less than hysteria.

One final question still remains to haunt the imagination.

[52] 37 Miss. at 250.

Why did the legislature go to the limit in 1842 and make it unlawful to "emancipate elsewhere"? What could it have mattered to Mississippi if an indeterminate but not overwhelming number of slaves were shipped to Liberia as freemen? Perhaps the answer to this question lies in that passage of the opinion in *Mitchell* v. *Wells*, where the court said: "[O]ur policy is opposed to the whole doctrine of negro emancipation, as at war with the interests and happiness of both races, . . . whatever tends to encourage emancipation, or to thwart the cherished policy of our State and people, or to establish the opposite policy, must be void." [53]

In short, as Mississippi struggled to preserve its peculiar institution against attacks from without, so slavery itself became more sacred and precious. As the assaults on slavery intensified, the very word "emancipation" came to symbolize the forces of evil working to destroy the institution. By 1859 there could be no middle ground between Negro slavery and white freedom. *Any* emancipation accommodation was anathema, and the explosive character of the high court's response merely testified to the loathsomeness of the idea in the minds of three men who had ceased deporting themselves like justices.

[53] *Ibid.*

CHAPTER V

The High Court Redeemed: Criminal Justice

The high court of Mississippi maintained in the area of criminal law such a dignity of stance and nobility of spirit that the antebellum court seems to emerge as a knighted institution in search of the Holy Grail of justice. Enlightened and well-reasoned, compassionate and yet scholarly, the cases flowing from the court in steady progression from 1822 to 1861 offer a refreshing change from the emancipation cases of Chapter 4, and they add up to an admirable body of criminal jurisprudence.

During this intensely creative period, the court gave vitality to those provisions contained in its own "Declaration of Rights" [1] which echoed the basic themes of the Fourth, Fifth, Sixth, and Eighth amendments to the United States Constitution. Unaided by any national criteria for measuring the specific content of justice or the elements of a fair trial, the Mississippi High Court found its answers after searching its own conscience and exploring the primary value of individual human dignity upon which the nation was founded. It was truly a court for all times.

Section 10 of article I of the constitution of 1832 contained the guarantees relating to procedural rights:

[1] The "Declaration of Rights" was article I of the constitutions of 1817 and 1832.

That in all criminal prosecutions the accused has a right to be heard, by himself, or counsel, or both; to demand the nature and cause of the accusation; to be confronted by the witnesses against him; to have compulsory process for obtaining witnesses in his favor; and in all prosecutions, by indictment or information, a speedy and public trial by an impartial jury of the county where the offence was committed; that he cannot be compelled to give evidence against himself, nor can he be deprived of his life, liberty, or property, but by due course of law.[2]

Freedom from unreasonable searches and seizures was guaranteed in section 9. The right to be proceeded against by indictment except in specified rare exceptions, the protection against double jeopardy, the prohibition against excessive bail, the right to bail, the privilege of the writ of habeas corpus, the prohibition against inflicting cruel punishments, and the inviolability of the right to trial by jury constituted the remaining individual safeguards of criminal law guaranteed by the constitution of 1832.[3]

By statute, the accused in a capital case was entitled to have "such counsel, not exceeding two, as [he] may desire" assigned to him by the court, upon his request, as well as a copy of the indictment, and a list of the special venire summoned on his trial, delivered to him at least two entire days before his trial. No provision for counsel was made for lesser offenses. In capital cases the defendant was also permitted twenty peremptory challenges to the jury, in non-capital, four; and he was entitled in capital cases also to a special venire consisting of one hundred persons.[4]

The cases applying these basic constitutional and statutory provisions exhibited at once a thoroughness in treatment of the

[2] The constitution of 1817 (art. I, § 10) contained the identical guarantees, with only two minor changes in wording.
[3] Miss. Const. art. I, §§ 9, 12–13, 16–17, 28.
[4] Ch. 48, § 16, ch. 49, §§ 17, 45, *Howard and Hutchinson's Digest* (1840), 667, 673; ch. 65, art. 2, §§ 49–50, art. 7, § 1, *Hutchinson's Code* (1848), 1003–1004, 1007; ch. 64 § 61, art. 294–95, 297, *Revised Code* (1857), 620–21.

legal principles involved and an acute sensitivity to the rights of the accused. Perhaps the most impressive quality of these early criminal cases, however, was the depth and range of legal scholarship. Mississippi justices had not only read the standard authorities on law, but were well acquainted with the decisions of other states. Without pretending to exhaustiveness, a few select cases from the whole body of criminal jurisprudence deserve attention; they typify the court's entirely rational approach to the issues raised, and at the same time illustrate its genuinely sympathetic attitude toward the accused.

In *Dyson* v. *State* [5] the defendant, James Dyson, shot and killed his enemy Samuel Helms after lying in ambush for Helms on a deserted country road. Tried on a murder charge, Dyson was found guilty of manslaughter. On appeal he argued that the record failed to set forth the full oath administered to the jury, and that this omission constituted reversible error, even though the record recited that the jury were in fact sworn. The high court affirmed Dyson's conviction unhesitatingly, but in its opinion it lingered over Dyson's objection and answered it as follows:

It is undoubtedly true, that the record must affirmatively show those indispensable facts, without which the judgment would be void,—such as the organization of the court; its jurisdiction of the subject-matter, and of the parties; that a cause was made up for trial; that it was submitted to a jury sworn to try it (if it be a case proper for a jury); that a verdict was rendered, and judgment awarded. Out of abundant tenderness for the right secured to the accused by our constitution, to be confronted by the witnesses against him, and to be heard by himself or counsel, our court has gone a step further, and held that it must be shown by the record that the accused was present in court pending the trial. This is upon the ground of the peculiar sacredness of this high constitutional right. It is also true, as has been held by this court, "that nothing can be presumed for or against a record, except what appears substantially upon its face." But this rule has reference to those indispensable requisites necessary to the validity of the record as a judicial proceeding, and can have no application to those incidental

[5] 26 Miss. 362 (1853).

matters which transpire during the progress of the proceeding in court.[6]

It would be difficult to quarrel with that studious effort to refute an objection which was weak at best—a mere "after-thought" in the word of the court.[7] Apparently Dyson overestimated his good fortune on the appeal after hearing the generous verdict of the jury.

After a verdict of acquittal upon a trial for theft, the district attorney of Hinds County applied to the high court for a writ of error in *State* v. *Anderson*.[8] Reasoning that to permit it would violate the double jeopardy provision of the state constitution, the court denied the application. "The adoption of the practice of permitting the State writs of error in criminal prosecutions," admonished Justice Thacker, "would work a vexatious hardship that is repugnant to the principles of criminal justice."

Double jeopardy had already received the attention of Mississippi's highest court in 1823 when that court assumed, in *State* v. *Moor*,[9] that this clause of the United States Constitution was binding upon the states as well, since "the Constitution of the United States is the paramount law of the land, any law, usage, or custom of the several states to the contrary notwithstanding." *Fox* v. *Ohio*,[10] holding that the prohibitions in the Fifth Amendment to the Constitution relating to criminal prosecutions were not designed as limits on the states but exclusively as restrictions on federal power, was not decided until 1847. In interpreting the Fifth Amendment, however, the Mississippi High Court held in the *Moor* case that jeopardy does not attach until after the rendition of the verdict of the jury, not from the moment of impaneling the jury:

The prisoner, it is said, was in jeopardy from the very moment the jury was empannelled to try him, but, I cannot persuade myself that such is

[6] *Ibid.*, 383.   [7] *Ibid.*, 384.   [8] 11 Miss. (3 S. & M.) 751, 753 (1844).
[9] 1 Miss. (Walk.) 134, 138 (1823) (grand larceny).   [10] 46 U.S. (5 How.) 410 (1847).

the fair construction to be given to the [fifth] amendment. The forms prescribed by the law, to ascertain the guilt or innocence of the accused, cannot properly be considered, that kind of jeopardy contemplated by the constitutien [sic] of the U. [sic] States; but, the means used by courts of law, in attaching the jeopardy, which can never take place, until after the rendition of the verdict by the jury, charged with the deliverance of the accused.[11]

Moreover, a conviction or acquittal on an invalid indictment is no bar to a second prosecution. That ruling came two years after *Moor* in the case of *State* v. *McGraw*,[12] where defendant was first indicted and tried on a charge of stealing a "negro man" and acquitted. A subsequent indictment for stealing a "negro man slave" withstood defendant's plea of double jeopardy. He had to stand trial again, since the appellation "negro man" in the first indictment was "insufficient to warrant a conviction."

Josephine v. *State* [13] established that in case of "legal necessity" a trial court does have the power to discharge a jury and order a mistrial without the consent of the defendant and before a verdict is entered, without violating the constitutional protection against double jeopardy. The circumstances surrounding the rule were unusual. Josephine and an accomplice, both slaves, were tried for murdering their mistress by adding arsenic to her afternoon tea. The jury announced precisely five minutes before the expiration of the November term that it could not agree on a verdict, whereupon the trial judge discharged the jury and declared a mistrial. At the following term of court Josephine was re-indicted, tried, and found guilty. Although the high court reversed her conviction on other grounds, it held that discharging the jury under those circumstances was a "legal necessity" which withstood a plea of double jeopardy. The ground on which the court reversed Josephine's conviction illustrates admirably its solicitude for the rights of the accused. The trial

[11] 1 Miss. (Walk.) at 139.   [12] 1 Miss. (Walk.) 208 (1825).
[13] 39 Miss. 613 (1860).

court had instructed the jury that she could be convicted of being an accessory before the fact upon an indictment charging her only as principal. "The matter involved here," said the high court, "was a substantial right of the prisoner and not a mere question of form of proceeding." [14] A new trial was ordered, but there is no further record of the case in the appellate court.

The meaning of the term "speedy trial" as used in the state constitution came before the Mississippi High Court in *Nixon* v. *State*, [15] a case evolving out of a habeas corpus proceeding heard in 1844. Charged with the murder of George Wiley, Nixon was indicted on Tuesday, March 21, 1843, and arraigned on Thursday, March 23, 1843. He then demanded that he be tried forthwith, but at the same time refused to waive his statutory right to examine a copy of the indictment *at least two entire days before* trial. In this impasse, the trial judge refused to try Nixon in that term of court because it was scheduled to adjourn on Saturday, March 25. If Nixon had been given his full two days to study the indictment as required by statute, he would have had only one day on which to go to trial, the last day of the term. This, in the opinion of the trial judge, was too short, and the high court agreed: "It [the trial] must, necessarily, have been precipitated with haste, and without that deliberation and reflection on the part of the court, which is due, as a right, in the course of law to an accused, in so solemn and awful a position." [16]

To Nixon's contention that he could not be tried at the following term because that would violate his right to a speedy trial, the high court replied:

Delays growing out of the established mode of proceeding, which has been so established by law, equally for the protection of the accused, and to accomplish the design of the scheme of laws, are evils necessarily attendant upon all human systems of jurisprudence. They are evils to which all may be subjected alike, and which constitute a part of the

[14] *Ibid.*, 647.   [15] 10 Miss. (2 S. & M.) 497 (1844).   [16] *Ibid.*, 508.

price paid for the advantages, far greater in proportion, thereby derived. By a speedy trial is then intended, a trial conducted according to fixed rules, regulations, and proceedings of law, free from vexations, capricious, and oppressive delays, manufactured by the ministers of justice.[17]

Nixon lost his fight and apparently went to trial, but again history gives us no clue of his eventual fate.

In *Murphy* v. *State* [18] the high court confronted the issue of the constitutional right of the accused "to demand the nature and cause of the accusation against him." [19] Defendant had been convicted of violating a statute of 1850 which made it a crime to trade and barter with slaves. However, the act allowed indictments under it to be framed without the name of the slave, or his owner, or the kind or quantity of the commodity bought or sold. Holding the act unconstitutional and simultaneously reversing Murphy's conviction, the court reasoned as follows:

The constitutional provision, that every man charged with a crime has a right "to demand the nature and cause of the accusation against him," was intended to secure to the accused such a specific designation of the offence laid to his charge, as would enable him to make every preparation for his trial necessary to his full and complete defence. We, therefore, think that under it the accused is entitled to demand "such a certain description of the offence charged, and statement of the facts by which it is constituted, as will fully identify the accusation, lest the grand jury should find a bill for one offence, and the defendant be put upon his trial for another, without any authority." [20]

A conviction of murder was reversed in *Mask* v. *State* [21] because it appeared from the record that the trial court had refused to permit any cross-examination to be made. It is especially noteworthy that the denial was on a hearing for a change of venue and the witnesses were merely expressing their opinions, as the court freely admitted, in regard to public sentiment. That factor, however, did not persuade the court to relax the constitu-

[17] *Ibid.*, 507.   [18] 24 Miss. 590 (1852).   [19] Miss. Const., art. I, § 10 (1832).
[20] 24 Miss. at 594.   [21] 32 Miss. 405 (1856).

tional guarantee. Said the court: "The rule on this subject is almost without exception, and is founded in both reason and the
clearest principles of justice, that an examination in chief of a
witness by a party, carries with it, the right to a cross-examination by the adverse party; the object being to elicit the whole
truth in regard to the particular subject of investigation before
the court." [22]

Not until 1859 did a case arise considering the privilege
against self-incrimination—*Newcomb* v. *State*.[23] Again the high
court seemed to believe that this provision of the Fifth Amendment was binding on the states. Defendant Tyra Newcomb was
indicted and convicted of the murder of John Freeze. At the
trial, Newcomb's mother testified as the chief witness for her
son. She was asked on cross-examination whether she had made
a statement after the murder of Freeze to the effect that if her
son did not kill John Freeze, she would disown him as her son.
Mrs. Newcomb did not claim the privilege against self-
incrimination, but rather answered the question by denying she
had ever made the statement. Defendant urged on appeal that
this question should not have been allowed because it tended to
implicate the witness in the killing. The high court affirmed the
conviction, ruling that the privilege must be claimed by the
witness personally:

> If this objection had been made by the witness, it might have ex-
> empted her from answering the question. But this is the privilege of
> the witness, given him by the law, and secured to him by the Constitu-
> tion for his own protection. It was the duty of the court to apprise him
> of his privilege—and that was done here—but not to prevent her from
> answering if she thought fit to answer, after being informed that she
> had the right to decline an answer.[24]

Then the high court went on to educate the bar on this point.
Any unfavorable inference which a jury might draw from a claim

[22] *Ibid.*, 426.   [23] 37 Miss. 383 (1859).   [24] *Ibid.*, 403.

of the privilege must be prevented by trial courts in proper instructions to the jury. The court continued:

This rule [that the question may be asked] does not appear to be affected by the provisions of Constitutions of the United States and of this State, that no party shall be compelled to give evidence against himself in a criminal prosecution. For he is not "compelled" to testify, under the rule as above stated, but may always protect himself by claiming his privilege; and this is the rule held by the courts in this country, notwithstanding the immunity secured to such persons by the Constitution of the United States, and of the States in which this rule has been held.[25]

Bail in capital cases was allowed on two occasions—in 1858 *Moore* v. *State* [26] and in 1861 *Beall* v. *State*.[27] The high court, in reversing the denial of bail by the trial court in each instance, reasoned that to allow it seemed "most consistent with the liberal policy of our Constitution and laws." In each case the special circumstance of the bad health of the defendant was present as a factor which probably persuaded the high court to decide as it did, and it proceeded to qualify its holding as follows: "We wish it understood, that on application for bail, we may grant the application, even in cases where the jury might, and perhaps, ought, on the same evidence, to render a verdict of guilty for murder. . . . we deem it unsafe, that the opinion of the High Court in granting or refusing bail should be adopted as a criterion for the jury, by which to determine the guilt or innocence of the accused." [28]

Bail after conviction was denied in *Ex parte Dyson*,[29] although the high court in affirming the trial court's ruling was careful to observe that the power is a discretionary one which will be exercised whenever "special circumstances" would justify it. No special circumstances warranted it in this case.

In construing the laws governing the selection of grand and

[25] *Ibid.*, 404.   [26] 36 Miss. 137 (1858).   [27] 39 Miss. 715 (1861).
[28] 36 Miss. at 142.   [29] 25 Miss. 356, 360 (1852).

petit juries, the high court consistently read the applicable statute with perfect literalness where such a literal reading would
inure to the benefit of the accused in a criminal prosecution.
One example of this practice occurred in *Leathers* v. *State*,[30]
decided in 1853. The high court there reversed a conviction for
assault with intent to commit murder on the ground that the
grand jury had been drawn from a greater number of persons
than provided by law (thirty-six being the legal number) and was
therefore void. Not the slightest doubt on this point crept into
the following language of the court: "A grand jury . . . does not,
by our law, consist of thirteen men congregated by the mere
order of court, or by accident, in a jury box; but it consists of the
requisite number of competent individuals, selected, summoned, and sworn according to the forms of law; and if the law
be not followed, it is an incompetent grand jury." [31]

However, in *Byrd* v. *State*,[32] the court, while affirming a conviction of a "free person of color" as an accessory before the fact
to the murder of a white man, held that the legislature could
constitutionally prescribe qualifications for those composing a
jury panel, even though the legislature could not abolish or
change substantially the panel or jury itself. Specifically the high
court upheld an act of 1830 requiring that jurors be "freeholders
or householders." [33]

A new trial was granted by the high court in at least two
cases [34] on the ground of the impartiality and incompetence of a
juror, who had formed an opinion in reference to the guilt or in-

[30] 26 Miss. 73 (1853).
[31] *Ibid.*, 77. In Carpenter v. State, 5 Miss. (4 How.) 163 (1839), the court reversed a
conviction for perjury where the record did not show that the jury consisted of twelve
men; and in Abram v. State, 25 Miss. 589 (1853), the court reversed a conviction for
murder where the record did not show that the grand jury had been sworn.
[32] 2 Miss. (1 How.) 163 (1834).
[33] Act of December 16, 1830, ch. 27, § 1, *Laws of Mississippi* (Jackson, Miss.: Peter
Isler, State Printer, 1830), 25.
[34] Cotton v. State, 31 Miss. 504 (1856); Alfred v. State, 37 Miss. 296 (1859).

nocence of the accused, which it would require testimony to dislodge, even though he might declare on his voir dire that he had no fixed bias in his mind either for or against the accused. In another case, *Sam* v. *State*,[35] in which a convicted murderer proved that one of the jurors had stated the day before his trial that "the prisoner should be hung," a new trial was also granted.

An interesting commentary on the high court's unyielding attachment to the constitutional right of trial by an "impartial jury" lies in the number of "death-oriented juries" drawn to try capital cases in antebellum Mississippi. As often as the issue arose, the high court steadfastly ruled that a proposed juror who evinced on his voir dire conscientious scruples against the infliction of the death penalty was not a competent juror and should be discharged.[36] Not even an assurance from the juror in *Williams* v. *State* on his voir dire that he thought he could do justice as between the state and the accused, gained a relaxation of the rule. In that case the high court said:

> The reason upon which this rule is founded is that such scruples entertained by a juror, incapacitate him as such, in the performance of his part in the due administration of the law. He must violate his conscience or disregard the obligations which the laws of the country attach to the relation in which he stands. There is no third course by which he can escape from *these* alternatives. If placed on the jury, he is compelled either to violate his oath or his conscience, and a man who would do either, is unfit to serve as a juror.[37]

Finally, in view of the frequency which the issue of misconduct of juries arose before the court as a basis for a motion for new trial, one is constrained to conclude that the security surrounding juries by bailiffs and trial judges in Mississippi must have been extremely lax. For example, in *Riggs* v. *State* [38] a

---

[35] 31 Miss. 480 (1856).
[36] Lewis v. State, 17 Miss. (9 S. & M.) 115 (1847); Williams v. State, 32 Miss. 389 (1856).
[37] 32 Miss. at 392.   [38] 26 Miss. 51 (1853).

convicted murderer alleged on his motion for new trial that the jury, while deliberating the case, ate at the public table of a hotel with a crowd of guests; that the landlord and servants of the hotel were freely admitted into their rooms; that the jury drank intoxicating beverages, played cards, and fiddled during the night; that the officer in charge went to sleep at 10:00 P.M. leaving the door unlocked; and that one of the jurors, without the consent of his officer, separated, and paid a matinal visit to his family. After granting defendant's motion the high court admonished in *Riggs:*

Irregularities on the part of juries impanelled and charged with the trial of felonies, and misconduct in the officers having them in charge have become of such frequent occurrence, that we deem it incumbent upon us, to suggest respectfully to the learned judges who preside in our circuit courts, that the corrective which they hold in their hands should be promptly and rigidly applied. It is manifest that if these evils which appear to be greatly on the increase, are not arrested, it must become in the end a vain effort to bring to just punishment any violation of the laws of the land.[39]

If it were not for the institution of slavery and the slave's unique status under the law, a study of criminal justice in Mississippi would lack the interest, as well as the complexity, which that institution gave it. The slave not only contributed to the richness of Mississippi's pre-Civil War criminal jurisprudence; in many of its aspects he provided the raw material out of which it was built. In a larger context the whole legal system of the state contained an ambiguity within a dichotomy in its approach to the slave. The dichotomy existed in the fact that under the civil

[39] *Ibid.*, 55–56. In Hare v. State, 5 Miss. (4 How.) 187 (1839), the court reversed a conviction for murder where a person who was not a sworn officer was permitted to go into the jury room after the jury had retired, and to have charge of them in the absence of a bailiff; and in Boles v. State, 21 Miss. (13 S. & M.) 398 (1850), the court reversed another murder conviction where, after the jury had retired, they were taken to a hotel and permitted to eat and consort with other persons in the hotel.

law, he was for most purposes a chattel,[40] a person rarely.[41] Under the criminal law he was usually deemed a person,[42] a chattel rarely.[43] The ambiguity arose from this double aspect of the slave under both the civil and the criminal law. Moreover, even if he was a person in the eyes of the criminal law, he was in a special category of persons which required a different code of laws for the regulation of his normal life, and particularly for the punishment of his criminal conduct.[44] "Experience has proved," said the Mississippi High Court in 1859, "what theory would have demonstrated, that masters and slaves cannot be governed by the same laws. So different in position, in rights, in duties, they cannot be the subjects of a common system of laws." [45]

[40] "Negroes, although persons for some purposes, are generally regarded as property, and excepted out of the general legislation in regard to persons, unless specially included. The color is *prima facie* evidence of liability to servitude. It is *prima facie* evidence of property in someone." Thornton v. Demoss, 13 Miss. (5 S. & M.) 609, 618 (1846).

[41] The importation of slaves into the state as merchandise was prohibited by the constitution of 1832. See Chapter 3 for a discussion of this problem and related issues in the civil law which revealed an awareness of the unique character of slaves as both persons and property by both the legislature and high court.

[42] "In prosecutions for offences, negroes are to be treated as other persons." Isham v. State, 7 Miss. (6 How.) 35, 42 (1841). The court held that a master was a competent witness for his slave on trial for murder.

[43] Where an injury was done to a slave by a third person, the master had a civil action of trespass to recover damages for the injury to the slave. Edwards v. Williams, 3 Miss. (2 How.) 846 (1838); Lamar v. Williams, 39 Miss. 342 (1860). Only where he committed murder upon a slave was a white man accountable under the criminal law for his conduct toward slaves.

[44] A detailed comparison of the criminal codes for the two races is beyond the scope of this work, but some general observations may be useful. In capital cases, the slave was assigned counsel by the court, if the master would not himself employ counsel. The cost was charged to the master, not to exceed $25.00. More "attempts" were made the subject of crimes for slaves than for whites and the death penalty was more usually attached. For a capital offense slaves were triable only in circuit court (the court of general jurisdiction). For all non-capital offenses, slaves were tried first before two justices of the peace and five slaveholders of the county where the crime was committed. If found guilty, the accused was granted the right of appeal to the circuit court and a trial de novo. Slaves were rarely sent to jail, punishment for non-capital offenses taking the form of whippings (thirty-nine lashes "well laid on"), branding, or the cutting off of an ear. The laws governing slaves were contained in *Howard and Hutchinson's Digest* (1840), ch. 11, pp. 153–81; *Hutchinson's Code* (1848), ch. 37, pp. 510–42; and the *Revised Code* (1857), ch. 33, pp. 234–56. See also Charles S. Sydnor, *Slavery in Mississippi* (New York: D. Appleton-Century Company, 1933), ch. 4.

[45] Minor v. State, 36 Miss. 630, 634 (1859).

Sometimes the legal dichotomy in treating slaves as both persons and property created an interesting conflict in a single case, where one or the other status had to yield. For example in *Doughty* v. *Owen*,[46] a slave was wanted for the crime of attempted rape. His master, Owen, sold the slave to Doughty after the crime and received a note from him for the price of the slave. In an action by Owen against Doughty on the note, the high court held the contract void. It reasoned as follows:

When a slave commits a crime, the private rights of the master must yield to the superior rights of the State, and he can only be influenced by those considerations which influence all good citizens, a fair and faithful administration of the law. The master can legally exercise no right which will interfere with the State in discharging her duty to society. . . .
. . . Any other rule would place the criminal code as to slaves completely at the mercy of their masters, and society could only be protected against the enormities of this class of our population in those cases in which the private interest of their masters would not be prejudiced by consenting that the law might be administered, and its penalties inflicted upon the guilty. The master himself has no such rights or exemptions from punishment if he commit crime. They occupy common ground.[47]

But always the legal dichotomy with its latent ambiguities reflected a profound tension, pervading the society as a whole, between a humanitarian, paternalistic concern for the Negro as a person—"a child just born" [48]—and an unsentimental regard for the same Negro as a chattel to be fought over in a litigious world.[49] Simply reciting the general rule that slaves were per-

---

[46] 24 Miss. 404 (1852).   [47] *Ibid.*, 407–409.
[48] Minor v. State, 36 Miss. 630, 633 (1859).
[49] Actions for specific performance lay to recover slaves in specie "from the peculiar character of slave property." Murphy v. Clark, 9 Miss. (1 S. & M.) 221 (1843). If an owner of slaves hired them out to a third person, he could not collect damages for an injury to them during the time of their hire, unless he proved an injury to his reversionary interest in the slaves. Lacoste v. Pipkin, 21 Miss. (13 S. & M.) 589 (1850). Runaway slaves were the subject of larceny. Randal v. State, 12 Miss. (4 S. & M.) 349 (1845); Coon v. State, 21 Miss. (13 S. & M.) 246 (1849). If a party had slaves in possession to which he supposed himself entitled, but which were decreed to other persons, he was liable to

sons under the criminal law did not always resolve particular
issues in concrete cases, however. Whether the immediate
problem concerned a crime committed by a slave, or a crime
committed upon a slave, the high court frequently found itself
facing a deeper philosophical question: Assuming that slaves
were accorded the status of persons under the criminal law, did
their rights under that law flow from their very nature as *persons*
(in which case, where the positive law was silent, all general
criminal laws would by implication apply to them) or, were their
rights created solely and exclusively by municipal law (in which
case none of the general criminal code would apply to them, in
the absence of a specific act bearing upon the point)? In the answer to that question sometimes lay the outcome of a case.
Three such cases will be analyzed, each presenting this problem
from a different angle.

In *State* v. *Jones* [50] a white man had killed a slave, but until
1821, the year of this decision, no one knew with certainty
whether the crime of murder could be committed by killing a
slave. If he was a natural person, as the criminal law held, it
would seem so; and yet, in the absence of a specific statute making the murder of a slave a crime, was it to be presumed that a
slave would receive the same protection of the criminal law as all
free white persons? Justice Clarke, writing an able and enlightened opinion, held that a crime had indeed been committed for
which the defendant would hang. Yet the court appeared to
reach its decision uneasily. It struggled with the implications of
holding to the contrary:

In this state, the Legislature have considered slaves as reasonable and
accountable beings and it would be a stigma upon the character of the

those who recovered them for the reasonable hire of the slaves since they came into his
possession, with a credit for the support of any slaves not worth their maintenance.
Newell v. Newell, 17 Miss. (9 S. & M.) 56 (1847).
[50] 1 Miss. (Walk.) 83 (1821).

state, and a reproach to the administration of justice, if the life of a slave could be taken with impunity, or if he could be murdered in cold blood, without subjecting the offender to the highest penalty known to the criminal jurisprudence of the country. Has the slave no rights, because he is deprived of his freedom? He is still a human being, and possesses all those rights, of which he is not deprived by the positive provisions of the law, but in vain shall we look for any law passed by the enlightened and philanthropic legislature of this state, giving even to the master, much less a stranger, power over the life of a slave. Such a statute would be worthy the age of Draco or Caligula, and would be condemned by the unanimous voice of the people of this state, where, even cruelty to slaves, much less the taking away of life, meets with universal reprobation. By the provisions of our law, a slave may commit murder, and be punished with death; why then is it not murder to kill a slave? Can a mere chattel commit murder, and be subjected to punishment? [51]

It argued that the positive law limited the rights of the master rather than conferred rights on the slave:

The right of the master exists not by force of the law of nature or of nations, but by virtue only of the positive law of the state, and although that gives to the master the right to command the services of the slave, requiring the master to feed and clothe the slave from infancy till death, yet it gives the master no right to take the life of the slave, and if the offence be not murder, it is not a crime, and subjects the offender to no punishment. [52]

But the court concluded by asking two questions, not entirely, one gathers, for rhetorical purposes:

The taking away the life of a reasonable creature, under the king's peace, with malice aforethought, express or implied, is murder at common law. Is not the slave a reasonable creature, is he not a human being, and the meaning of this phrase *reasonable creature* is a human being, for the killing a lunatic, an idiot, or even a child unborn, is murder, as much as the killing a philosopher, and has not the slave as much reason as a lunatic, an idiot, or an unborn child? . . . And shall this court, in the nineteenth century, establish a principle, too sangui-

[51] *Ibid.*, 84.   [52] *Ibid.*, 85.

nary for the code even of the Goths and Vandals, and extend to the whole community the right to murder slaves with impunity? [53]

It will be noted that *Jones* reasoned, in essence, that the taking of life was murder at common law, and since the slave is a reasonable creature, the common law should govern. Much later, in 1859, the Mississippi High Court was to consider the problem in a different framework. Specifically, *George* v. *State* [54] raised the issue whether it was a crime for a slave to rape another slave. In holding that no crime had been committed, the court rationalized that "slaves . . . having no rights prior to legislative enactment, to the municipal law alone we must look for all their rights." Since no statute embraced either the attempt or actual commission of a rape by a slave on a female slave, the indictment for such an offense was considered a nullity. Neither the common law nor statutory law, stated the court decisively, extended to or included slaves, either to punish or protect them, unless they were specifically named. To underscore its points, it referred to the rationale of *Jones*, namely, that the common law extended ex proprio vigore to slaves, as "unmeaning twaddle." [55]

The result here stands out in sharp contrast to that reached in the third case of the series, *Wash* v. *State*, [56] decided in 1850. In that case a slave was indicted in two counts for (a) the commission of a rape upon a white child under ten and (b) an attempt to commit a rape upon the same child. At the time the crime was perpetrated, no statute covered this precise situation since the statutory crime of rape in the general criminal code (count one of the indictment) was held not to cover slaves, and the actual commission of a rape by a slave upon a free white woman or child was, incredibly, not an offense under the slave code. It was, however, a capital offense for "any slave to *attempt* to com-

[53] *Ibid.*, 85–86.   [54] 37 Miss. 316 (1859).   [55] *Ibid.*, 318–20.
[56] 22 Miss. (14 S. & M.) 120, 124 (1850).

mit a rape on any free white woman or female child under the age of twelve years." [57]

Furthermore, section twenty-one of the general criminal code stated that "no person" could be convicted for an attempt if the actual crime attempted was completed,[58] and the evidence seemed to prove that Wash did complete the crime. This seemed to knock down count two of the indictment. Clearly there was a gap in the law. Yet, the trial jury returned a general verdict of guilty and the trial court pronounced the death penalty. The question in the high court was raised, therefore, whether the trial court could pronounce any judgment at all in this predicament. In affirming Wash's conviction, the high court first ignored the evidence pointing to the actual completion of the crime and thereby neutralized the effect of section twenty-one. It then reasoned that while the indictment was "irregular," an attempt was necessarily included in the commission of the offense, and if the jury found him guilty of the larger offense, judgment could be entered for the lesser, which was the death penalty anyway. Not entirely a sound argument in view of the statutory structure, to be sure, but sufficient to affirm the conviction. The court could hardly have permitted a statutory oversight to enable a black slave to rape a white girl and escape scot free.[59]

In *Minor* v. *State* [60] the court again considered the opposing theoretical views: i.e., one, that a slave was a person only to the extent that he was relieved of his status as a slave and expressly recognized as such by positive legislative enactment, or two, that he was entitled to all the rights accorded to persons under the criminal law simply because he was first a person. That case raised the immediate issue whether a slave could appeal to the

---

[57] Ch. 37, § 55, *Hutchinson's Code* (1848), 521.   [58] Ch. 64, § 21, *ibid.*, 983.
[59] Ch. 33, § 11, art. 58, *Revised Code* (1857), 248, plugged this gap and made rape by a slave upon a white woman or child a capital crime.
[60] 36 Miss. 630 (1859).

high court a decision of the circuit court (the court of general jurisdiction) affirming his conviction for the non-capital offense of grand larceny by two justices of the peace and five slaveholders.[61]

Defendant argued that the general language of the criminal code extending the right of appeal to the high court to all criminal cases [62] embraced the trials of slaves in justice courts. Rejecting the argument, the court held that the decision of the circuit court was final and not subject to review by the high court. Its opinion emphasized the strict dichotomy existing between the two systems of criminal justice:

> In this State, the legislature has adopted a code, with express reference to the trial of slaves, defining the offences, from murder to the lowest offences; affixing penalties; establishing a special tribunal for their trial, wholly differing in its character from the mode applied to persons who are citizens; regulating the competency of witnesses—how summoned—the mode of compelling their attendance; and providing for the keeping and preservation of its records and papers, and for fees and costs, and, finally for appeal to the Circuit Court.
>
> It can hardly be supposed, therefore, that, in the great number, variety, and minute particularity of the provisions, establishing a *system*, having reference to this class alone, it could have escaped the scrutiny of the legislature, if they had so intended, to make provision for writs of error also; and the fact, that in an act, so carefully considered and making such important changes, no provision for writs of error to this court is made is strongly persuasive that none was intended.[63]

If the appeal were allowed in this class of case, reasoned the court, slaves would be allowed three distinct trials, while "the

[61] For all non-capital offenses, slaves were tried first before two justices of the peace and five slaveholders of the county where the crime was committed. If found guilty, the accused was granted the right of appeal to the circuit court and a trial de novo. Ch. 33, § 12, arts. 68–77, *Revised Code* (1857), 250–52.

[62] "The high court of errors and appeals, or any judge thereof in vacation, or any judge of the circuit court, shall grant writs of error and supersedeas *in all criminal cases,* under the restrictions provided in this section." (Italics added.) Ch. 64, § 63, art. 306, *Revised Code* (1857), 622.

[63] 36 Miss. at 635–36.

superior race, the white man, has no such right extended to him in cases of the greatest magnitude by our laws."

But the genius of the decision lay in the court's rejoinder to defendant's argument that slaves were *persons* under the criminal law and that the unqualified language of the criminal code extended to them too: "Generally, it would seem, that an act of the legislature, would operate upon every person within the limits of the State, both natural and artificial. Yet, when the provisions of a statute evidently refer to *natural* persons, the court will not extend them to *artificial*." [64]

By thus distinguishing between artificial persons and natural persons, Justice Harris was able to resolve on an intellectual level the person-chattel conundrum of the criminal law. In practice, however, the two separate "systems" of criminal justice referred to in *Minor* often broke down as a particular justice, caught between the two legal realms in which the slave existed as both chattel and person, leaned over to the view which looked at the slave as a natural-born person under the law, not as an artificial person created for limited purposes.

Isham v. *State* [65] considered the question whether a master could give evidence on behalf of his slave on trial for murder, and Chief Justice Sharkey answered it affirmatively with an appeal to "justice" without even attempting to construe or reconcile the applicable statutes. He asked:

What would be the condition of the slave, if that rule, which binds him to perpetual servitude, should also create such an interest in the master, as to deprive him of the testimony of that master? The hardship of such a rule would illy comport with that humanity which should be extended to that race of people. In prosecutions for offences, negroes are to be treated as other persons; and although the master may have an interest in his servant, yet the servant had such an interest in the testimony of the master as will outweigh mere pecuniary considerations;

[64] *Ibid.*, 634.   [65] 7 Miss. (6 How.) 35 (1841).

nor could he be deprived of the benefit of that testimony by the mere circumstance that, in a civil point of view, he was regarded by the law as property.[66]

Justice Clayton took an even stronger position in *Lewis* v. *State*,[67] where the admission of a dying declaration of the deceased slave in a murder trial of another slave was objected to on the ground that slaves did not possess a sense of religious accountability. The justice, after observing that "by statute, all the laws in force for the trial of a free white person, for a capital offence, are declared to be in force for the trial of slaves for offences declared capital by the laws of this state," [68] held the dying declaration admissible, saying:

It is true that if the declarant had no sense of future responsibility, his declarations would not be admissible. But the absence of such belief must be shown. The simple, elementary truths of christianity, the immortality of the soul, and a future accountability, are generally received and believed by this portion of our population. From the pulpit many, perhaps all who attain maturity, hear these doctrines announced and enforced, and embrace them as articles of faith. We are not inclined to adopt the distinction.[69]

In the matter of resistance and rebellion, the law was equally ambivalent. "Unconditional submission and obedience to the *lawful* commands and authority of the master is the imperative duty of the slave," said the high court in *Oliver* v. *State*,[70] and accordingly the "master may use just such force as may be requisite to reduce his slave to obedience, even to the death of the slave, if that becomes necessary to preserve the master's life or to maintain his lawful authority." In that case a master has been convicted of the manslaughter of his slave John. The evidence at the trial showed that John was a huge, mean-tempered, rebellious slave who frequently refused to follow orders. On the day

[66] *Ibid.*, 42.   [67] 17 Miss. (9 S. & M.) 115 (1847).
[68] *Ibid.*, 119. Justice Clayton was quoting from ch. 40, § 12, *Hutchinson's Code* (1848), 483.
[69] 17 Miss. at 120.   [70] 39 Miss. 526, 540 (1860).

of the homicide Oliver, the master, attempted to take from the slave a five-foot-long stick (used for shelling corn). When John refused to yield the stick to his master, a tussle ensued, and John lost. A blow to the head sent him to the floor where he died moments later. On this evidence, the high court reversed the conviction and sent the case back for a new trial with proper instructions to the trial court on the law of resistance and rebellion. Although the court went on in dicta to say that "if, without necessity, or apparent necessity, in reducing his rebellious slave to subjection, the master wantonly take his life, he would certainly be guilty of murder or manslaughter," the hard rule of law to be derived from *Oliver* was that a master might kill his slave "in self-defence, or in the exercise of necessary and lawful force in order to secure obedience." [71] It was for the jury to decide whether the degree of force used was or was not excessive under the circumstances.

In *Kelly* v. *State* [72] there are dicta to the opposite effect, namely, that "the attempt to take the slave's life, by the master, or any other, feloniously, may rightfully be resisted by him." However, in that case no issue squarely presented itself to test this alleged right of resistance. The facts are lacking except for the information that the case involved an indictment of a white man for the murder of a slave and a conviction of manslaughter. The high court reversed and remanded on other grounds.

A test of the right to resist acknowledged in *Kelly* came in 1859 in *Wesley* v. *State*. [73] A slave being tried for the murder of his overseer attempted to prove in his defense of justifiable homicide that the deceased had generally managed the plantation "with reference to violence and cruelty" and had committed "specific acts of unmerciful severity" on him and other slaves while acting as overseer. The court in affirming the conviction

[71] *Ibid.*, 539–40.   [72] 11 Miss. (3 S. & M.) 518, 526 (1844).
[73] 37 Miss. 327, 346 (1859).

held proof of the general management of the plantation and evidence of specific acts of violence inadmissible where they were not part of the *res gestae*. The following rationale is of particular interest in showing the basic orientation of the court on this particular issue:

> If the slave, when he is about to be chastised, or has just reason to apprehend that he will be subjected to cruel and unmerited punishment, be informed, that in order to escape, he may innocently slay his master or overseer if he really believes that by the apprehended punishment his own life will be taken or greatly endangered; and that to make good his defence in a court of justice, it will be sufficient to prove the general violent and cruel conduct of the deceased in the government of slaves; the slave population of the State will be incited to insubordination and murder, and the life of the master exposed to destruction, either through the fears or by the malice of his slaves.[74]

Thus, where a contrary holding would have threatened the very structure of society and the position of the whites as rulers of that society, the court carefully applied a rule of law which conformed to the accepted social philosophy and at the same time crippled the right of resistance. Unfortunately, no other case arose which tested that right.

The law of confessions was literally forged out of the institution of slavery, and, ironically, it was in this area where Mississippi's greatest contribution to criminal justice lay in the period before the Civil War. Across a span of twenty-six years and a cluster of cases involving capital crimes committed by slaves, a body of law evolved which would be considered enlightened even by contemporary standards. The ambiguities and the tensions were absent here. One trend of policy and one thread of law ran through the cases, and that was to engraft as many restrictions on the use of confessions in court as were necessary, not only to protect the individual accused from physical abuse, but also to protect the criminal law itself from possible debase-

[74] *Ibid.*, 348–49.

ment by specious appellate doctrine rationalizing a bare pretense of justice at the trial level.

As early as 1835, in *Serpentine* v. *State*,[75] the high court reversed a conviction of murder on the ground that the confession of the accused slave had been coerced by a severe lashing inflicted on the accused by a group of local citizens. The following paragraph from the court's opinion speaks for itself:

It also appears from the exceptions taken at the trial, that the counsel for the defendant offered several witnesses who were not permitted to be sworn, to prove, that during the night preceding the examination before the magistrate, the witnesses who were then offered, went to the house of the late John Dubois, where finding the prisoner, they took him from his bed, bound him to a tree, and while naked, he was whipped by four persons seccessively [*sic*], that having suffered the severest inflictions of the lash, "he was told to confess about the murder of Dubois." [76]

Such a confession was not admissible in evidence against the defendant under a "rule of law," said the court, "universally recognized to be founded, not only on dictates of humanity, but upon the soundest principle of reason." [77]

In 1844, in *Peter* v. *State*,[78] also a murder case, the high court raised the presumption of law that the influence of a threat or promise once made continues to operate, and accordingly, a second confession made without first warning the accused of its consequences, was held inadmissible. In its opinion the court exhibited a special solicitude for the accused as slave:

Being a slave, he must be presumed to have been ignorant of the protection from sudden violence, which the presence of the justice of the peace afforded him, and he saw himself surrounded by some of those before whom he had recently made a confession. As we gather from the whole record, he then reiterated his previous confession. This court has before, under similar circumstances, refused to acknowledge such confessions as evidence [citations omitted]. It is true, that by

[75] 2 Miss. (1 How.) 256 (1835).   [76] *Ibid.*, 257.   [77] *Ibid.*, 260.
[78] 12 Miss. (4 S. & M.) 31 (1844).

adopting this rule the truth may sometimes be rejected; but it effects a greater object, in guarding against the possibility of an innocent person being convicted, who from weakness has been seduced to accuse himself, in hopes of obtaining thereby more favor, or from fear of meeting with immediate or worse punishment. We conclude that, as the facts are disclosed in the record, the confession was improperly admitted in evidence.[79]

The confession in question had been obtained after a mob had collected at the house of the now dead owner of the slave and threatened the black with death by immediate hanging. Armed with guns, the mob later escorted the frightened suspect to the justice of the peace, to whom he confessed. This doctrine of exclusion was affirmed in *Van Buren* v. *State*,[80] where a slave had been whipped into confession.

The court hammered out another rule in *Jordan* v. *State* [81] by holding that the protection against self-incrimination extends against violence used by private individuals as well as to compulsion exercised by officers of government to obtain a confession of guilt:

The State being powerless as to this mode of procuring testimony, can give no countenance or sanction to a similar mode, when employed by individuals. The power which restrains the State, equally restrains her citizens in this respect. To hold otherwise would not unfrequently expose the accused to the excited passions or fury of that class of population who in all countries are the subjects upon whom the criminal jurisprudence of the government can be most beneficially employed.[82]

In that case, the slave Jordan was convicted of the murder of another slave. At the trial, one Mallory, introduced as a witness for the state, testified that after the killing he and another white man accosted the accused and threatened to kill him if Jordan did not confess. Jordan promptly confessed to every detail. The court as promptly threw out the confession and granted a new trial.

[79] *Ibid.*, 38–39.   [80] 24 Miss. 512 (1852).   [81] 32 Miss. 382 (1856).
[82] *Ibid.*, 387.

An instruction to the jury that a confession is to be regarded as the "highest and most satisfactory character of proof" was held erroneous and the conviction of manslaughter reversed in *Brown* v. *State*.[83] The language of that instruction gave "too great weight to this species of evidence" and failed to draw any distinction between "deliberate" and "casual" confessions.

The rule that confessions made after "very slight" expressions promising a benefit or escape from punishment are inadmissible was repeated and applied in *Simon* v. *State*.[84] In that case Simon confessed to the murder of another slave after his pursuer, Ellis, had admonished him that "you had better tell the whole truth about the matter." A slave named Hiram was missing and a possible suspect. Later in the day Simon confessed again in front of Ellis and his master. In pronouncing the confession tainted, the court overcame the state's argument that nothing was said to the accused to induce him to confess to his own guilt as follows:

That position is, that nothing was said to the accused to induce him to make confessions of his own guilt; that he was only required to tell the truth in relation to the guilt of the boy Hiram; and that he was told that "he had better tell the whole truth" in relation to Hiram's act in the matter. Conceding that this was the purport of what was said to him before he made the confessions, still, it does not obviate the objection, that he was thereby placed under intimidation, and induced to make the confessions which he did make. The confessions are presumed to have been made in consequence of the appeal to his hopes and fears, and cannot, therefore, be said to be the act of his own free will, and entitled to be taken as evidence against him.[85]

Finally, *Stringfellow* v. *State*,[86] a case involving murder committed by a white man, established that an accused could not be convicted of a capital felony by the extra-judicial confession of the prisoner where the corpus delicti was not proven by in-

[83] 32 Miss. 433, 450 (1856).   [84] 37 Miss. 288 (1859).   [85] *Ibid.*, 294.
[86] 26 Miss. 157 (1853).

dependent testimony. In one of its most scholarly opinions, the court reviewed exhaustively the state of the law on this subject, and concluded with the following comment:

> This question is one of first impression in this court; and its importance has induced us to bestow upon it the greatest deliberation which circumstances would permit. We believe that the doctrine which holds that, in capital felonies, the prisoner's confession, when the *corpus delicti* is not proved by independent testimony, is insufficient for his conviction, best accords with the solid principles of reason, and the caution which should be applied in the admission and estimate of this species of evidence.[87]

It should not be assumed, however, that all confessions were excluded. Where the court was satisfied from the record that the confession was made voluntarily, it was admitted and the conviction affirmed. For example, in *Frank* v. *State* [88] the defendant argued, on appeal from a conviction of burglary, that he had confessed to the crime while another slave was being whipped in his presence "in relation to matters connected with the burglary." The high court was not impressed. It believed that the record showed the whipping to have been given for disobedience, not for the purpose of inducing Frank to confess.

Moreover, acts of the accused done in consequence of an inadmissible confession and tending to show guilt were admissible. This was the rule of *Belote* v. *State.* [89] There, defendant confessed under pressure from the owner to the larceny of ten bank bills. He then walked to the place where he had hidden the bills and produced them to the owner of the bills. Defendant vainly objected at the trial to the introduction of the testimony relating to the production of the ten bank bills. The court reasoned as follows:

> In such cases, it is not the confession of the party that is received in evidence against him, but the facts which are brought to light by his

[87] *Ibid.*, 165.   [88] 39 Miss. 705 (1861).   [89] 36 Miss. 96 (1858).

acts and in consequence of the confessions. It will not do to say that the acts having been brought about by improper means, are of the same character as confessions produced by the same means; that the influence which produced groundless confessions might also produce groundless conduct; for when the acts of the accused point out and produce the stolen property in its place of concealment, that fact speaks for itself, and is inconsistent alike with the idea of falsehood and innocence.[90]

A further qualification held that a confession made by a slave to his master did not fall within the rule of privileged communications, and was properly admissible, if free and voluntary. Thus, in *Sam* v. *State*,[91] Sam confessed to his master that he had burned the gin and cotton house on his master's plantation. The court reasoned:

Such confessions are not incompetent upon any sound legal principle; and to establish the rule that they are incompetent, would be highly impolitic and dangerous; because, from the nature of the connection between master and slave, if confessions fully made to him should not be admissible, they would not be likely to be made to any others; and thus, however true the confessions, and however strongly corroborated by circumstances, all violations of law committed by slaves, the proof of which depended on that sort of evidence, would go unpunished in the courts of justice.[92]

It is not difficult to assign reasons why the law of confessions took on the character of a careful solicitude for the accused—in particular, the accused slave. Confessions were too easily extracted from him, and the possibilities for abuse were infinite. Only a vigorously protective policy on the part of the high court could counteract the tendency to "overwork" the use of the confession by local authorities and private individuals acting in concert. Furthermore, no strong public policy militated against according to the slave the highest degree of legal protection from coerced confessions, as was true in *Wesley* v. *State*, with its overtones of threatened insurrection, and in *Wash* v. *State*,

[90] *Ibid.*, 118.   [91] 33 Miss. 347 (1857).   [92] *Ibid.*, 352.

where a serious crime would have gone unpunished on account of a legislative oversight.

The foregoing discussion can be reduced to three main propositions:

1. Excluding its contacts with slavery, criminal justice in antebellum Mississippi developed into a precociously liberal phenomenon as it was molded by a high court which evinced a rather pronounced belief that the Mississippi courts should tolerate no unfair prosecution.

2. In its approach to slavery the criminal law, excluding confessions, straddled two legal concepts imbedded in the society as a whole: one which regarded slaves as property, the other as persons. This duality gave the law an uncertain, querulous quality symptomized by a frequent use of the rhetorical question in the opinions of the high court.

3. In the law of confessions, the liberality of white criminal justice was extended to the slaves; the duality in the law disappeared, and justice became a single, coherent concept.

CHAPTER VI

In Purgatory: The High Court and Reconstruction

When the Mississippi High Court grappled with the legal problems engendered by reconstruction, it turned to the United States Supreme Court for guidelines in an area of law where precedents were few indeed. So few were the precedents, in fact, that perhaps the best approach to judicial reconstruction in Mississippi would be to isolate *Texas* v. *White*,[1] decided by the Court in 1868, as the watershed case, and then arrange for analysis the Mississippi cases according to their distance in time and theory from that landmark. What *Texas* v. *White* contributed to the substantive law of reconstruction will be considered at some length later in the chapter. For the present, its importance can be conveyed in a single sentence. It provided the Mississippi appellate justices, who were anxiously awaiting a pronouncement on the subject from the nation's highest court, with an authoritative theory of reconstruction and a simple rule which they could apply at the state level in deciding their own cases.

Not that there was a dearth of reconstruction constitutional doctrine at the national level; on the contrary, in the political sector there were perhaps too many theories competing for na-

[1] 74 U.S. (7 Wall.) 700 (1868).

124   DEFENDER OF THE FAITH

tional acceptance without any one even pretending to universality. From the indulgent "presidential theory" of Andrew Johnson, which held that the southern states had never been out of the Union at all, to the punitive "conquered province" theory of Thaddeus Stevens, which held that they should now have to apply for admission to the Union as new states, a constitutional explanation sprouted to match every shade of the political spectrum represented in Congress. But, cautiously, the Supreme Court of the United States bided its time. If, then, the Supreme Court waited until 1868 to speak out on reconstruction theory, and if it spoke but once in a major case, which virtually defined its role in the drama of reconstruction, what were the issues coming before the Court which occupied its time during this period?

To an important degree the cases adjudicated concerned the validity and effect of legislation passed by the seceded states and the Confederate Congress during the period of the "rebellion." In a smaller measure the cases passed on the validity of executive actions, including those of military commanders, during the actual conduct of hostilities.[2] Only a few involved the constitutionality or interpretation of acts of Congress embodying some phase of early reconstruction policy.[3] Only the first category is

[2] The Prize Cases, 67 U.S. (2 Black) 635 (1862), upheld the action of the president in blockading southern ports in 1861; The Grapeshot, 76 U.S. (9 Wall.) 129 (1869) upheld the power of the president, as commander-in-chief, to establish provisional courts in insurgent territory occupied by Union forces during the war.

[3] Mrs. Alexander's Cotton, 69 U.S. (2 Wall.) 404 (1864) construed the abandoned property act of March 12, 1863 to require that property captured during the rebellion be turned over to the Treasury Department to be sold by it and the proceeds deposited in the National Treasury, so that any person asserting ownership of it might prefer his claim in the Court of Claims. Miller v. United States, 78 U.S. (11 Wall.) 268 (1870) upheld the constitutionality of the confiscation acts of August 6, 1861, and July 17, 1862, as an exercise of the war powers of the government. United States v. Klein, 80 U.S. (13 Wall.) 128 (1871) interpreted these same acts so as not to confiscate or absolutely divest the property of the original owner, even though disloyal. By the seizure the government constituted itself a trustee for those who were entitled or whom it should thereafter recognize as entitled.

relevant to this study. By examining the issues touching the validity and effect of state wartime legislation as they were refracted through one particular state court, it is possible to view the subject of judicial reconstruction in both its macro and micro dimensions, to appreciate the impact of reconstruction on the internal life of Mississippi as well as in its relations with the federal government.

Internally, the impact had its physical and psychological aspects; both were equally turbulent, equally traumatic. A ravaged land lay in a state of shock under the footprint of federal military power. The war was over but the aftermath had yet to be endured, and that was worse because the glory was gone. During this agony of spirit which Mississippi experienced, especially between 1865 and 1870 (the year of its readmission to the Union), there arose and then festered an obsessive concern with the nature of the state's identity during the Confederacy and under reconstruction. If one had to reduce that concern into its component parts, it could be stated as a paradox within a dilemma. The dilemma consisted of a desire to be recognized both as a belligerent power and a legitimate state of the Union. Perhaps no more galling words to the southern ear during the Reconstruction Era were those which told him that nothing had been accomplished in 1861, that it was all a futility, an action null and void.

Amidst the ruins of war this was unbearable, and thus grew one horn of the dilemma: the need to have the deed recognized for what it was—a brazen and nearly successful attempt to perpetuate an institution and split a nation. Yet this yearning had to be reconciled somehow to the other side of the organism—that which longed to revert to the status quo without trauma and agony, and which inclined toward the view that the process of "restoration" was simply a matter of slipping back into the Union, minus the slaves, and picking up where things left off in

1861. The paradox is contained in the apparent contradiction between a theory of reconstruction which denied any fundamental change in the state's relation to the federal government and the obvious presence of federal military power in occupied Mississippi.

Nowhere are this paradox and that dilemma more sharply etched than in the debates of the constitutional convention of 1865. Called by Provisional Governor William L. Sharkey in his proclamation of July 1, 1865, for the purpose of amending the old state constitution of 1832 to accord with the realities of life in 1865, that convention spent an inordinate amount of time and energy dwelling on the subject of the state's identity before, during, and after the Confederacy as well as on the precise degree of sovereignty the convention enjoyed. In point of fact, however, the only concrete accomplishments of the convention were the abolition of slavery in Mississippi and the repeal of the Ordinance of Secession.[4]

Moreover, the dilemma and the paradox were perceived not only in the constitutional convention, but also in the early reconstruction cases decided by the Mississippi High Court. Turning to that court and its role during the political-constitutional crisis, one is able to discern a three-layered pattern. Phase one begins in 1866 when the high court resumed activities after the close of the war; it continues through the period usually designated as "presidential reconstruction" and ends with the resignation of Chief Justice Handy in October, 1867. The theory of reconstruction employed by the high court in this initial phase may be termed the "public enemy" theory, the major premise of the cases being that a full-fledged de facto government existed in Mississippi during secession with the authority to enact legislation which survived the Confederacy.

Phase two begins with the judicial reaction to "congressional

---

[4] *Journal of the Proceedings and Debates in the Constitutional Convention of the State of Mississippi, August, 1865* (Jackson, Miss.: E. M. Yerger, State Printer, 1865), 35, 37.

reconstruction" occurring in 1869 with the case of *Thomas* v. *Taylor*,[5] decided by the high court which General Edward Ord had appointed in 1867. Briefly, the thesis of the *Taylor* case and its progeny was that the government of Mississippi from 1861 to 1865 was a revolutionary band and its acts mere nullities in contemplation of law—the "big void" theory.

Phase three begins with the newly styled "Supreme Court of Mississippi" organized in the spring of 1870 following the adoption of the constitution of 1869. This final period is characterized by the pragmatic approach of the court to the issues generated by reconstruction. The cases, furthermore, show the benign influence of *Texas* v. *White*, which restored cool reason to the judicial aspect of reconstruction where mainly emotion had prevailed before.

Hill v. *Boyland*[6] is the leading case which expounded the "public enemy" theory. The issue concerned the validity of an act of the Mississippi legislature of January 29, 1862, suspending the statute of limitations until twelve months after the close of the war. In holding the act to be valid, the court used two different theories. One was derived from the law of nations, and the other was essentially the indestructibility-of-states theory of reconstruction constitutional law (also known as the "southern" theory, or the "presidential" theory of Andrew Johnson). The court reasoned in the first phase of the opinion that the Confederacy had acquired belligerent rights during the Civil War; its territory was treated as enemy territory, its citizens as "public enemies." The government of the Confederacy had a de facto status, and within the territorial limits of Mississippi "there remained a regularly organized government *de jure*, as well as *de facto* which was never disputed."[7] Speaking directly to the

[5] 42 Miss. 651 (1869).   [6] 40 Miss. 618 (1866).

[7] 40 Miss. at 637. For authority the court quoted the famous lines of Grier, J., in the Prize Cases, 67 U.S. (2 Black) 635, 673–74 (1862):

> Hence, in organizing this rebellion, they have *acted as States* claiming to be sovereign over all persons and property within their respective limits, and asserting a

point of the internal character of the state during hostilities, the court said:

But the proposition, that the citizens, who owed at least temporary allegiance to the government which possessed their property, and controlled by its power their persons, during the period of such dominion, were remanded to a state of nature as barbarians and outlaws—in all their relations with each other, civil as well as criminal—as a judicial question, seems to us neither sanctioned by the principles of international law, recognized by our highest judicial tribunals, nor by any code of morality known to civilized nations.[8]

As for the effect in fact and law of the Ordinance of Secession, "the attempt to change her relations towards the United States Government only involved her external relations." For, according to *Hill*, the result of the war impressed upon the state, insofar as her internal affairs were concerned, a character analogous to that of a conquered nation in international law, and "the subsequent resumption of authority by the former sovereign cannot change the character of *past transactions*, or deprive the citizens of rights vested under the laws of the territory while it was permanently *possessed* and *governed* by the enemy as their territory." [9]

In short, under the law of nations the municipal laws of a conquered territory remain in force "until altered by the newly created power of the State." Ergo, the act suspending the statute of limitations is valid until altered by "the new sovereign." So ended one half of the argument establishing the unimpaired

---

right to absolve their citizens from their allegiance to the Federal Government. Several of these States have combined to form a new confederacy, claiming to be acknowledged by the world as a sovereign State. Their right to do so is now being decided by wager of battle. The ports and territory of each of these States are held in hostility to the General Government. It is no loose, unorganized insurrection, having no defined boundary or possession. It has a boundary marked by lines of bayonets, and which can be crossed only by force—south of this line is enemies' territory, because it is claimed and held in possession by an organized, hostile and belligerent power.

[8] 40 Miss. at 627.   [9] *Ibid.*, 628, 637.

vitality of domestic legislation in the state during its absence from the Union. The other side of the coin—the one reasserting Mississippi's perpetual ties to the Union—is even more provocative and the two together form an irresistible combination. The court glided gently into its new course with the following passage, so pregnant with meaning that its full import does not become apparent at the first reading: "But 'the belligerent right of the United States Government, growing out of the suppression of the rebellion, does not confer on it the *right of conquest* after the suppression. No nation can make a conquest of its own territory. It acquires no new title, but only regains the possession, of which it was temporarily deprived.' " [10]

What the court goes on to prove from language taken from Justice Sprague in *The Amy Warwick* [11] is that the "conquered nation" status has no application to the external character of the state after the war in its relations to the federal Union. "In legal effect, the character of Mississippi as a State in the Union was . . . established and not destroyed by the events of the war and the act in question remains unaffected by its political results." [12] Thus, since the state of Mississippi never ceased to exist, all its acts were valid unless in conflict with the Constitution. The preservation of the Union assured by the northern victory proved that the state could never have been anywhere else, nor could it be anywhere else now except in the Union. This rationale satisfied, of course, the longing to be recognized as both a belligerent power and a legitimate state at once. Either argument, whether derived from international or constitutional law, led to a desirable resolution of the concrete issue in the case while both lines of reasoning were congenial to the prevailing southern mentality. It could not have been a more agreeable combination of ideas.

[10] *Ibid.*, 634, 639.   [11] 1 F. Cas. 808 (No. 342) (D.C.D. Mass.) 1862.
[12] 40 Miss. at 639.

In the same term *Murrell* v. *Jones* [13] was also decided on the "public enemy" theory. At issue was the validity of a contract founded on the consideration of Confederate money, made in the city of New Orleans after its surrender to the Union army but prior to the date of the military order prohibiting its circulation (May 27, 1862). Applying principles of international law and citing *Hill* v. *Boyland* and a series of pre-reconstruction Supreme Court cases of the early 1860s, the high court held for the validity of the contract, summing up the rationale in the following passage:

> These adjudications save us the trouble of any argument upon the subject, and fully establish the proposition, that on the 3d of May, 1862, New Orleans was enemy territory to the United States, that its inhabitants were enemies, that they were not entitled to the protection of the Constitution and laws of the United States, or to sue in their courts; and that therefore their own municipal laws remained in force, as they did immediately before the conquest, except so far as they had been abolished or changed by the conqueror. [14]

Curiously, what the court in *Hill* had denied as a theoretical proposition, namely, that the belligerent rights of the United States government could "confer upon it the right of conquest after suppression," had actually been already recognized as a practical fact six months before *Hill*, in *Scott* v. *Billgerry*. [15] That case faced squarely the paradox inherent in a theory of reconstruction which could deny any fundamental change in the constitutional posture of the state while federal military power obviously ruled in Mississippi.

The question in *Scott* concerned, first, the power of the provisional governor to create a special court of equity on July 12, 1865, and second, the jurisdiction of that court. Again, the high court's decision looked in two different directions, as the external pressure created by the presence of federal troops met an in-

---

[13] 40 Miss. 565 (1866).   [14] *Ibid.*, 578–79.   [15] 40 Miss. 119 (1866).

ternal pressure to assert the continued sovereignty of the state. To the first question the court gave an answer which confronted the paradox directly. After conceding that the provisional governor derived his authority from the president himself as the commander-in-chief ruling over "conquered territory," the court said:

The aspect of the case, in any sound view of the constitutional relations between the States and the Federal government, would be different. Assuming the doctrines of those who supported the cause of the Union, none of these belligerent rights existed after the close of actual hostilities. It was maintained by them that a State had no right to separate from the Union, and that the people of the Confederate States were rebels in arms against their rightful sovereign. The war waged against the people of these States could be justified on no other theory—for if the right to withdraw existed, the war was a flagrant wrong—and the logical deduction from the premise was, that the relations of the States to the Union suffered only a temporary derangement, and that upon the suppression of armed resistance to the National authorities, the States immediately and necessarily resumed their normal position as States in the Union, and fell at once into their regular movements in their former orbits. Such a result, however inevitable it may have seemed, was not allowed to be realized, and we have been subjected to the ordinary rules of warfare and conquest, as they exist between distinct and independent nations. However inconsequential this may be, and however inconsistent with the principles and purposes avowed in the prosecution of the war, to wit, the indissolubility of the Federal Union, and the compulsory restoration of the seceding States, *nevertheless the facts exist in a form that defies logic, and we have no choice but to accept the condition actually impressed upon us by superior power*, and to govern ourselves by the rules and principles applicable to such cases.[16]

But having accepted the factual presence of military power, the court could not resist the pressure from within to confront that power with a resistance of its own. It held on the second point, regarding the jurisdiction of the special court, that it had no jurisdiction to enforce specific performance of the contract in

[16] *Ibid.*, 134–35 (emphasis added).

question since it was not such a contract as equity courts generally enforce by a decree of specific performance (even though the provisional governor had conferred such jurisdiction upon it), and that such exercise of power violated the Seventh Amendment to the federal Constitution providing for the right to trial by jury in cases at common law. Here is the interesting language of the high court on this second issue:

Without disputing the power of the Executive of the nation, while holding a State under absolute military rule, to create provisional governments, to ordain laws, and to establish judicial tribunals for their administration, still, all these powers must be exercised in subordination to the Constitution of the United States. That instrument recognizes the distinction between legal and equitable rights, and when the President, or his subordinates, undertake to create civil tribunals to administer the laws of any State or Territory, held for the time being under military dominion, he is bound to respect these fundamental regulations, and to refrain from exercising a power which the legislative department of the government would not, in the same case, possess. He may abstain from instituting civil tribunals, if he will; but if he exercises the power, he cannot disregard the restrictions of the organic law. [17]

In 1867, the case of *Harlan* v. *State* [18] continued the theory of *Hill, Murrell,* and *Scott.* The court in *Harlan,* instead of showing frustration at the paradox, found comfort, as the court in *Hill* had found, in the tidy thought that either theory—the "public enemy" theory of international law or the indestructibility-of-states theory under constitutional law—led to the same decision in that case. The problem was whether a criminal indictment found on December 4, 1865, for a felony committed on May 30, 1865 (before the appointment of the provisional governor) was valid, or to put it in broader terms, "whether on the 30th day of May A.D. 1865, the State of Mississippi had any legal and valid existence as a State." To pose the question was to answer it:

[17] *Ibid.*, 143.   [18] 41 Miss. 566 (1867).

We entertain no doubt, that the laws of the States, civil and criminal, as they stood at the date of the secession ordinance, continued in force afterwards, precisely as before, unaffected by that ordinance, or by the war, or by the deposition of the State magistrates in the month of May, 1865, or their restoration in the fall of that year; and that offences against the criminal laws, committed during the war, or during the occupation of the State by the army of the United States, are now liable to indictment and punishment as if these events had never occurred. [19]

Furthermore, this proposition was true "whether we adopt the theory that prevailed at Washington during all the progress of the war, that the Union is indestructible, the ordinances of secession absolutely void, and that the seceding States never did or could cease to be States of the American Union; or the theory that has grown up since the return of peace, that such States are conquered territory, subject to the laws of war." [20]

Indeed, there had been utterances from the United States Supreme Court itself which seemed to support the belief that the "theory that prevailed at Washington during all the progress of the war" would prevail thereafter. In *The Venice*,[21] property libeled as a prize of war was restored to its former owner in New Orleans because it had been wrongfully seized after the permanent occupation of that city by federal troops. The Court had said, in dicta, that as far as possible, the people of such parts of the insurgent states as came under national occupation and control, were treated as if their relations to the national government had never been interrupted. And in referring to certain proclamations of military commander Major-General Benjamin Butler, issued upon his entry into the city, the Court reiterated this theme: "Both [proclamations] were the manifestation of a general purpose which seeks the re-establishment of the national authority, and the ultimate restoration of States and citizens to

[19] *Ibid.*, 569.   [20] *Ibid.*   [21] 69 U.S. (2 Wall.) 258 (1864).

their national relations, under better forms and firmer guaranties, without any views of subjugation by conquest." [22]

Such dicta, of course, predated the enactment of the Reconstruction Acts.[23] What vitiated the theory referred to in *Harlan* was the crisis between President Johnson and Congress over reconstruction policy, which had been simmering and finally boiled over in Washington, while the Mississippi High Court was registering its consternation over the incompatibility between theory and fact in *Scott* v. *Bilgerry*. That crisis, however, was not yet even in the making at the time of the *Venice* dicta in 1864. The words were uttered in good faith; they simply proved to be a weak base from which to project one's views as to the future direction of reconstruction policy.

Before the doctrinal change occurred on the Mississippi High Court in 1869, which signified the necessity of revising the state's reconstruction theory to harmonize with the shift at the national level in 1867, the state court quietly operated, for the most part, from the precedent of *Hill* v. *Boyland* and its progeny, upholding the validity of transactions effectuated during the Confederate administration. It was not always necessary, of course, to reargue the propositions of that case, derived as they were from both principles of international law and a particular view of constitutional law. It was usually simpler and more direct to reach a desired result in a given case on the ground of public policy, leaving the theory of *Hill* as the unspoken major premise. This was especially true in a line of cases originating in *Green* v. *Sizer*,[24] all having to do in some form with the enforceability of private contracts made during the rebellion founded on the consideration of "cotton money," "Confederate money,"

---

[22] *Ibid.*, 277–78.
[23] There were four Reconstruction Acts in all: Act of March 2, 1867, ch. 153, 14 Stat. 428; Act of March 23, 1867, ch. 6, 15 Stat. 2; Act of July 19, 1867, ch. 30, 15 Stat. 14; Act of March 11, 1868, ch. 25, 15 Stat. 41.
[24] 40 Miss. 530 (1866).

or Mississippi treasury notes.[25] Upholding the validity of such contracts, the court in *Green* reverted to the distinction between the private rights of individuals and the *"political status* of the seceded states." It could find "no reason of public policy which demands that rights of private property, acquired [during the war], should be disturbed; and there are strong reasons of justice and sound policy why they should be treated as fixed rights, and should have the protection of law." [26]

The court in *Cassell* v. *Backrack* [27] reached the same conclusion in upholding the validity of a title under a tax sale in 1864, its language, however, reflecting the passage of the Reconstruction Acts:

> Whilst we admit that the public policy of the United States government holds that the Confederacy and the State governments organized thereunder were unlawful combinations, and their acts illegal and void so far as they affect that government and its loyal citizens; still in reference to all matters of internal, private and domestic import, indifferent to the government and laws of the United States, we are satisfied it is our duty to hold that so far as the inhabitants of the Confederacy were concerned, it was a government in fact for the time being, for the purpose of conserving fully the private rights of persons and property, and for the protection of individuals from liability and punishment for obeying the laws of such government. To hold differently, would overturn, without particularizing, almost every transaction, whether of a public or private nature, which transpired during the supremacy of the Confederacy, and would lead to consequences productive of incalculable mischief.[28]

Where, however, the parties to the contract were respective citizens of the Confederate and United States during the Civil War, the contract was not only held void but usually denounced in strong moralistic tones. *Shotwell* v. *Ellis & Co.* [29] and *Sprott* v. *United States* [30] present an interesting pair of cases on this

---

[25] Frazer v. Robinson, 42 Miss. 121 (1868); Beauchamp v. Comfort, 42 Miss. 94 (1868); and Holt v. Barton, 42 Miss. 711 (1869).
[26] 40 Miss. at 556.   [27] 42 Miss. 56 (1868).   [28] *Ibid.*, 69–70.
[29] 42 Miss. 439 (1869).   [30] 87 U.S. (20 Wall.) 459 (1874).

point. Although they both reached the same conclusion in avoiding the transaction, *Shotwell*, the Mississippi case, reasoned from the premise that it was a contract "between the subjects of separate belligerent powers, and as such [they] were enemies." [31] Therefore, it was void as violative of both public policy and an act of Congress forbidding all intercourse between them. [32] *Sprott*, the Supreme Court case, considered rather the Confederacy to be a "treason respectable only for the numbers and the force by which it was supported." [33] Yet both were equally vehement in condemning the nature of the transaction in similar language. Consider the following passage from the opinion of the court in *Shotwell:*

> Why do the courts refuse their aid to parties who have entered into contracts which are *mala in se* or *mala prohibita?* It is not because of any tenderness or regard for the feelings or supposed rights of the contracting parties, but for the reason that they will not lend their assistance to parties *so defiled.* They are morally and legally regarded as being so *unclean* that the courts will not touch them, nor will they allow themselves to be touched by any such parties. They are banished outlaws from the halls of justice, and will not be permitted to approach and pollute its unsullied fountains. [34]

In *Sprott*, the Supreme Court said a few years later:

> That any person owing allegiance to an organized government, can make a contract by which, for the sake of gain, he contributes most substantially and knowingly to the vital necessities of a treasonable conspiracy against its existence, and then in a court of that government base successfully his rights on such a transaction, is opposed to all that we have learned of the invalidity of immoral contracts. A clearer case of turpitude in a consideration of a contract can hardly be imagined unless treason be taken out of the catalogue of crimes. [35]

Another duet of cases—this pair bringing the United States Supreme Court and the Mississippi High Court together—arose over the issue of liability to the owner for the destruction of

[31] 42 Miss. at 441.   [32] Act of July 13, 1861, ch. 3, § 5, 12 Stat. 257.
[33] 87 U.S. (20 Wall.) at 463.   [34] 42 Miss. at 443.   [35] 87 U.S. (20 Wall.) at 463.

property by the military during hostilities. In *Ford* v. *Surget* [36] the Mississippi court held that the owner could not recover from one Surget, who had burned Ford's cotton while Surget was acting under orders from General P.G.T. Beauregard, on the ground that "whatever might be rightfully done in a foreign war by a belligerent in the prosecution of hostilities could be done by the Confederates. . . . The defense is complete when it is ascertained that the burning of the cotton was a hostile, belligerent act in obedience to military order." [37]

The case went up on a writ of error to the Supreme Court under the same designation, *Ford* v. *Surget*. [38] The Court affirmed the Mississippi judgment relieving Surget from civil responsibility in an opinion by Justice Harlan which again emphasized a point in its rationale different from that relied on by the Mississippi court. One of the arguments advanced by the defense was that an act of the Confederate Congress of 1862 had authorized the burning of cotton by the military to prevent its falling into enemy hands. In fact, defendant Surget recited this statute in his pleadings and argued it in his brief. In disposing of the statute, Justice Harlan said, after holding that the destruction was justified purely as an act of war: "We do not rest this conclusion upon any authority conferred or attempted to be conferred upon Confederate commanders by the statute of the Confederate congress, recited in the special pleas. As an act of legislation, that statute can have no force whatever in any court recognizing the Federal Constitution as the supreme law of the land." [39]

In truth, the Mississippi court had not quite overlooked the statute in question. It too had said that "the law itself was no justification, the act could only be excused when accomplished by a 'vis major.' " [40] However, the difference was not just a matter of

---

[36] 46 Miss. 130 (1871).   [37] *Ibid.*, 155.   [38] 97 U.S. 594 (1878).
[39] *Ibid.*, 604.   [40] 46 Miss. at 153.

emphasis, since in holding first on the issue of jurisdiction to hear the case, the Supreme Court said:

> The defendant, Surget, justifies his burning of the cotton under military orders, issued by a Confederate general, in pursuance of authority conferred by an act of the Confederate congress. If we regard substance rather than mere form or technical accuracy, the defence rested upon that act, the validity of which was, in terms, questioned by the several demurrers to the special pleas. The general orders of the State court overruling the demurrers must be accepted, in every essential sense, as an adjudication in favor of the validity of an act of the Confederate congress, recognized and enforced as law in Mississippi, and which act, according to the rule laid down in that case, must be, therefore, regarded by us as a statute of that State, within the meaning of the provisions of the act declaring the appellate jurisdiction of this court. It results that we have power to review the final judgment of the Supreme Court of Mississippi.[41]

Thus, because the Mississippi court had overruled the demurrers raising the question of the validity of any defense predicated on an act of the Confederate Congress, the United States Supreme Court, in the posture of the case as it came up before it, deemed that the state of Mississippi had enforced and given effect in Mississippi the Confederate statute relied on by Surget in his defense. This procedural error explains why the Supreme Court went out of its way to squelch the statute as a defense in precise and explicit terms, even though the Court needed the statute to give it jurisdiction in the matter.

To walk into the cases beginning with *Thomas* v. *Taylor* is to enter another doctrinal world. Whereas *Hill* v. *Boyland* and its successors had upheld certain state wartime legislation on the legal ground that the state had at least a de facto existence with a de facto government during the war, *Thomas* v. *Taylor* worked hard to invalidate other types of state war legislation on the legal premise that the Mississippi government from January 9, 1861, to the appointment of the provisional governor on June 13,

[41] 97 U.S. at 603–604.

1865, simply did not exist in contemplation of law. Secession had created neither a government de facto nor de jure; it left only a big void, which no amount of casuistry could explain away.

At issue in *Thomas* was the validity of the Mississippi treasury notes and "cotton money" issued during the war, which figured in the contract case of *Green* v. *Sizer*, among others. The state legislature had provided that these notes should be receivable in payment of taxes. After the organization of the provisional government in July, 1865, these treasury notes and "cotton money" were tendered in payment of taxes due the provisional government. The high court held that the provisional government was not bound by the obligations of the government that existed in the state during the war, and could not be compelled to receive the treasury notes and "cotton money"; it ruled that the notes had been issued in aid of the rebellion and were void. If the case of *Hill* v. *Boyland* were not already in the jurisprudence of the state, the court might not have labored so hard to eradicate the government founded on the Ordinance of Secession. But it had much to overcome in undoing the rationale of that case. Burrowing its way from the ground up, the court began with a disquisition on the character of the American system of government. For the first time in the constitutional history of the state were written the following words:

The Constitution of the United States is not merely a league of sovereign States, for their common defence against external and internal violence, but a supreme federal government, acting not only upon the sovereign members of the Union, but directly upon all its citizens in their individual and corporate capacities. . . . There is nowhere to be found the slightest allusion to the instrument as a compact of States in their sovereign capacity, and no reservation of any right, on the part of any State, to dissolve its connection, or to abrogate its assent, or to suspend the operations of the Constitution as to itself.[42]

[42] *Ibid.*, 697–98.

Having laid to rest the dogma of secession as a constitutional right, the court proceeded to a consideration of the government operating during secession, and found that it was "a government without any connection with or dependence on the government of the United States." Its perfect severance of any constitutional tie to the United States was underscored in the following language:

What the government of the State of Mississippi, a member of the Confederate States, did, from the passage of the ordinance of secession in 1861 to the surrender of the Confederate armies in 1865, cannot with any propriety be said to have been done by the government of the State of Mississippi, one of the United States. When that ordinance passed, there ceased to be within the State, a government under the Constitution of the United States.[43]

The character of that "government" from the point of view of the United States was described as follows:

The government of the United States has uniformly, from early in 1861 to the spring of 1865, characterized the controlling authorities of those seceded States not as governments, but as unlawful combinations of rebellious persons, usurping the functions of government, and forcibly controlling the people. That government has invariably regarded them as parts of a machinery for waging unlawful war, and making treasonable resistance to the rightful authority of the United States, having their central power in the government of the Confederate States, and co-operating in one combination for the unlawful and treasonable purpose of overthrowing by force of arms the Constitution of the United States.[44]

In response to the de facto argument of *Hill* v. *Boyland*, the Mississippi court said:

Neither the government of the Confederate States nor the several governments of any of the States, composing the Confederacy can properly be said to be a de facto government, from the date of secession to the overthrow of the Confederate government. . . . It was only what it

[43] *Ibid.*, 702.   [44] *Ibid.*, 702–703.

professed to be—a revolutionary organization, seeking to establish a Confederacy of States, and dependent wholly for success upon the success of the revolution.[45]

Gradually, it worked its way into the heart of the issue with the preface that "government is the ligament that holds the political society together, and when that is destroyed, the society as a political body is dissolved." Then it was ready for the climax:

Thus the debts of a society are cancelled when the society perishes; though the members, whilst the society subsisted, were jointly bound to contribute towards the payment of the public debts, this obligation will cease when the society subsists no longer. . . .
The laws of the insurrectionary government ceased when that government was overthrown. They had no legal authority, and had only the authority which force gave them, and when that yielded, the laws enacted by the unlawful government ceased to have any operative force as to the future.[46]

Finally the high court concluded with one of the strongest statements to be found in any case of this period: "The rebellion, in its revolutionary progress, having *deprived the people of the State of Mississippi of all civil government*, the President of the United States, in order to avert the manifold evils consequent upon a state of anarchy, assumed to initiate the means for reorganizing a civil government for the people of the State." [47] This was tantamount to stating as a fact what the court in *Cassell* v. *Backrack* had so solemnly denied: "This tribunal will take judicial notice of the fact as a matter of public notoriety and history, that the inhabitants of the Confederacy were not reduced to an absolute condition of barbarism, anarchy, and chaos during the continuance of the rebellion." [48]
The judicial body totally ignored the doctrine which the Mississippi Supreme Court was to state two years later in *Leachman*

[45] *Ibid.*, 703.   [46] *Ibid.*, 706–707.   [47] *Ibid.*, 709.   [48] 42 Miss. at 69.

v. *Musgrove* [49] to be an imperative of governmental secession: "It is absolutely necessary, when one government succeeds another, that there should be no vacuum, no interregnum, otherwise, for a time, there might be an absence of authority, resolving society into a condition of chaos and anarchy."

Thomas went up to the United States Supreme Court in 1874, but while affirming the Mississippi decree, the Court wrote a lacklustre opinion. The only vivid language in the opinion is the opening paragraph:

> Beyond all doubt the finding of the appellate court of the State of Mississippi is correct, and the court here also unanimously concur in the conclusion reached by that court, that the treasury notes authorized to be issued by the act under consideration, inasmuch as they were issued "against the public policy and in violation of the Constitution of the United States, are, therefore, illegal and void." [50]

Now, it is obvious from the virulence of the language of *Thomas* v. *Taylor* that the Mississippi High Court went much further in espousing a radical theory of reconstruction than was necessary in order to hold the treasury notes invalid.[51] One explanation for the abrupt shift in constitutional theory regarding the status of the seceded states accomplished in *Thomas* lies, of course, in the complete change in the high court's composition which occurred in October, 1867, following the resignation of all three "secessionist" justices upon the coming of congressional reconstruction to Mississippi. Alexander H. Handy, William L. Harris, and Henry T. Ellet, elected to the court on October 2,

---

[49] 45 Miss. 511, 536 (1871). The Leachman case concerned the transition from military to civilian government in 1870. It held that military appointees in Mississippi in office on February 23, 1870, continued to hold over until the abolition of their respective districts and dispensation with their services (by act of the legislature of April 22, 1870 creating fifteen new circuit court districts), and their right to compensation continued until that date.

[50] Taylor v. Thomas, 89 U.S. (22 Wall.) 479, 486 (1874).

[51] Interestingly, both courts totally ignored the fourth section of the Fourteenth Amendment (adopted July 28, 1868), which states that "neither the United States nor any State shall assume or pay any debt or obligation incurred in aid of insurance or rebellion against the United States."

1865, during the brief interlude known as presidential reconstruction, were all secessionists. The three men resigned simultaneously on October 1, 1867, in protest against the erection of
military government in Mississippi under General Edward Ord
shortly after the passage of the Reconstruction Acts of 1867. The
members of the court appointed by General Ord [52]—
Shackleford, Peyton, and Jeffords—were all Republicans or Re-
publican sympathizers; moreover, they must have believed fer-
vently in the policy behind the Reconstruction Acts. Otherwise
the extreme language and tone of the opinion, epitomized by
the statement that the rebellion deprived the people of Mississippi during the period of the rebellion of all civil government,
are incomprehensible. [53]

Certainly *Thomas* v. *Taylor* went far beyond the rationale of
Texas v. *White*, handed down just a year before by the Supreme
Court of the United States. That case faced the question
whether the state of Texas had ever been out of the Union during its attempted secession. The facts were rather involved. In
1850, the United States had given the state of Texas $10 million
in 5 percent bonds in settlement of certain boundary claims.
Half were held in Washington; half were delivered to the state
and made payable to the state or bearer, redeemable after December 31, 1864. A Texas law was passed providing that the
bonds should not be redeemable in the hands of any holder until
after their endorsement by the governor. Texas joined the
Confederacy at the outbreak of the Civil War, and in 1862 the
state legislature repealed the act requiring the endorsement of
the bonds by the governor and created a military board to pro-

---

[52] This court survived only until the reorganization of the high court in 1870 under the
constitution of 1869, when it became the "Supreme Court of Mississippi."

[53] The Preamble to the Reconstruction Act of March 2, 1867 designated as "Rebel
states" all of the Confederacy except Tennessee, and declared that "no legal State governments or adequate protection of life or property existed there." Act of March 2, 1867, ch.
153, 14 Stat. 428.

vide for the expenses of the war, empowering the board to use any bonds in the state treasury for this purpose up to $1 million. In 1865 the board made a contract with White and others for the transfer of some of the bonds for military supplies. None of the bonds was endorsed by the governor of the state. Immediately upon the close of the war, but while the state was still "unreconstructed," suit was brought by the governor of the state to get the bonds back and to enjoin White from receiving payment for them from the federal government.

At the very outset of the case the question arose whether Texas, unrestored to its normal status as a member of the Union, was still a "state" within the meaning of article III of the Constitution, extending the original jurisdiction of the Supreme Court to those cases "in which a state shall be a party." The opinion seems quite mild after reading *Thomas* v. *Taylor*. In holding that Texas could maintain its action because it had never ceased to be a state of the Union, the Supreme Court of the United States also called the government of Texas under its Ordinance of Secession "unlawful": "It [the legislature of Texas] cannot be regarded, therefore, in the courts of the United States, as a lawful legislature, or its acts as lawful acts." [54]

But in the very next sentence the Court qualified that negative as follows:

And, yet, it is an historical fact that the government of Texas, then in full control of the State, was its only actual government; and certainly if Texas had been a separate State, and not one of the United States, the new government, having displaced the regular authority, and having established itself in the customary seats of power, and in the exercise of the ordinary functions of administration, would have constituted, in the strictest sense of the words, a *de facto* government, and its acts during the period of its existence as such, would be effectual, and, in almost all respects, valid. And, to some extent, this is true of the actual government of Texas, though unlawful and revolutionary, as to the United States. [55]

---

[54] 74 U.S. (7 Wall.) 700, 732–33 (1868).   [55] *Ibid.*, 733.

The Court had already devoted a considerable part of its opinion to proving the proposition that the state of Texas, as distinct from its government, had never ceased to be a state in the Union:

> When, therefore, Texas became one of the United States, she entered into an indissoluble relation. All the obligations of perpetual union, and all the guaranties of republican government in the Union, attached at once to the State. The act which consummated her admission into the Union was something more than a compact; it was the incorporation of a new member into the political body. And it was final. The union between Texas and the other States was as complete, as perpetual, and as indissoluble as the union between the original States.[56]

Far from ending on a note which branded the condition of a seceded state during its absence as a "state of anarchy," thus implying that none of its acts was valid, the United States Supreme Court judiciously drew the line of reason and good sense between those acts which were void and those which were not:

> It is not necessary to attempt any exact definitions, within which the acts of such a State government must be treated as valid, or invalid. It may be said, perhaps with sufficient accuracy, that acts necessary to peace and good order among citizens, such for example, as acts sanctioning and protecting marriage and the domestic relations, governing the course of descents, regulating the conveyance and transfer of property, real and personal, and providing remedies for injuries to person and estate, and other similar acts, which would be valid if emanating from a lawful government, must be regarded in general as valid when proceeding from an actual, though unlawful government; and that acts in furtherance or support of rebellion against the United States, or intended to defeat the just rights of citizens, and other acts of like nature, must, in general, be regarded as invalid and void.[57]

Such a line of demarcation had actually been implicitly recognized as long ago as *Hill* v. *Boyland*, except that the distinction there was enmeshed in a now discredited theory. The criterion erected in *Texas* v. *White* for determining the validity of any given act, contract, or transaction—i.e., that acts in aid of the

<hr>

[56] *Ibid.*, 726.   [57] *Ibid.*, 733.

rebellion were void, but those pertaining to purely private matters valid—became the rule which future courts were to follow. It was thus possible by 1870 for the Mississippi Supreme Court in *Buchanan* v. *Smith*,[58] in applying the rule to uphold the act of 1862 suspending the state statute of limitations, to cite both *Hill* and *Texas* as authority.

Thomas v. *Taylor* was not quite reduced to an anomalous freak of Mississippi jurisprudence, however. Like *Hill*, it bore a line of descendants which inherited its qualities, although to a much less marked degree. *Mississippi Central R.R.* v. *State* [59] held that a debt due the lawful government of Mississippi was not discharged by payment to the revolutionary government on the theory that "the government of the state of Mississippi of the United States was not the government of the state of Mississippi of the Confederate States." In *Buck* v. *Vasser* [60] the court refused to honor an auditor's warrant for salary due from the insurrectionary government to a district attorney who had rendered his services to that government, on the ground that

. . . said warrants were issued in payment of a salary claimed by relator as an officer of the late illegal government temporarily set up in the state of Mississippi, in violation of the constitution of the United States and in rebellion against the government thereof; that said illegal government having been overthrown and abolished by the power of the United States, all its debts and obligations perished with it.[61]

The court concluded with the following bit of advice: "For his salary while in the service of that illegal undertaking, he must look to the 'unlawful combination of rebellious persons usurping the functions of government, and forcibly controlling the people.' Loss of salary in such service is one of the trifling penalties attached to the 'unlawful combination.' " [62]

And *Bailey* v. *Fitz-gerald* [63] reluctantly overruled an earlier Mississippi decision [64] to hold invalid a statute of 1861, which

[58] 43 Miss. 90 (1870).   [59] 46 Miss. 157, 215 (1871).   [60] 47 Miss. 551 (1873).
[61] *Ibid.*, 555.   [62] *Ibid.*, 559.   [63] 56 Miss. 578 (1879).
[64] Trotter v. Trotter, 40 Miss. 704 (1866).

authorized guardians to invest their wards' money in Confederate bonds. The court ruled the statute invalid as being in aid of the rebellion, and held the guardian personally accountable in 1867, when the bonds were worthless, to his ward for mismanagement of funds. Only the authority of a Supreme Court decision could have compelled such a result, as the Mississippi court freely conceded:

> Since that decision [*Trotter* v. *Trotter*] the Supreme Court of the United States, in *Horn* v. *Lockhart,* 17 Wall. 570, had the precise question before it, under the Alabama statute, and held that such investment of the trust funds contributed to the financial resources of the Confederate government, and was in aid of its cause, and that neither the statute nor the judgment of the Probate Court could give it any validity. The language of the Court was, "that no acts of the Convention, *no judgment of its tribunals,* and no decree of the Confederate government could make such transaction lawful."
>
> . . . .
>
> We are constrained to follow the decisions of the Supreme Court of the United States in these adjudications.[65]

In 1876, *Shattuck* v. *Daniel* [66] went so far as to hold that "all taxes imposed and collected during that period for military purposes, were illegal," and, therefore, that the state of Mississippi acquired no title to land sold to it under a tax sale in 1862 for delinquent taxes due in 1861. What gives this decision particular significance is the court's refusal to entertain an argument advanced by the state in a proceeding to confirm its title, that some of the taxes collected were not in aid of the rebellion, but were rather levied for legitimate purposes. In answering the point the court said: "The rule is that where there are divers [*sic*] taxes all must be legal, otherwise the sale is void. It follows that the state acquired nothing by the purchase at the sale of 1862." [67]

---

[65] 56 Miss. at 589–90.   [66] 52 Miss. 834, 838 (1876).

[67] *Ibid.* See also State v. McGinty, 41 Miss. 435 (1867), denying the state a right to maintain a cause of action against a surety on the bond of a tax collector who collected taxes in 1861 to aid the rebellion, on the ground that the tax statute was a nullity; and

No case after *Thomas* v. *Taylor*, however, adopted the radical position assumed there or wrote in the style of that opinion. As time wore on, the sole issue before the court seemed to be whether or not the particular contract, statute, or transaction in question was or was not in aid of the rebellion, and not whether the state of Mississippi or its insurrectionary government existed de facto, de jure, or not at all. Metaphysical theory gave way to the application of a rule of practical reason. The court in *Shattuck* summed up the shift in emphasis as follows:

> Immediately succeeding the close of the war there was much discussion in the courts, federal and state, as to the *status* and functional authority of the insurgent states after the overthrow of the federal authority, and before its restoration. The United States did not, in either its political or judicial departments, recognize any validity in the acts of secession, or any rightful legal authority as vested in the confederate government. Various and incongruous theories were put forward by jurists and judges. The times were not then propitious for calm and unimpassioned juridical discussions, and, as a consequence, inconsistent and conflicting resolutions were announced by judges.
>
> But each discussion, especially when conducted with calmness, has contributed some light upon the subject, until now the judiciary of the country, federal and state, seem to agree with almost unanimity in the doctrine that all the public organized acts of the insurgent states—legislative, executive and judicial—done after the overthrow of the national authority within their respective limits, are valid, if within the limits of the state power, unless repugnant to the constitution of the United States, the laws passed in pursuance thereof, or in aid of the war against them.[68]

Thus the supreme court [69] had no qualms about holding in *Whitney* v. *State* [70] that a seller of firearms to the state in 1860 could recover from the state on his contract in a suit brought

---

Files v. McWilliams, 49 Miss. 578 (1873), holding that an overpayment of taxes in 1862 could not be recovered in 1873, as the amount overpaid was for the support of the war.

[68] *Ibid.*, 837.

[69] The designation reflects the renaming of the state's appellate court accomplished by the constitution of 1869.

[70] 52 Miss. 732 (1876).

after the war, although it was argued by the state, in defense, that the arms had been furnished to aid the rebellion. Without any theoretical excursions, the court came directly to the point:

There is nothing whatever in the position that the payment of the debt sued on is prohibited by those clauses of the state and federal constitutions which forbid the assumption or payment of debts contracted in aid of the rebellion. The act authorizing the purchase of the arms in question was passed on 15th of December, 1859, and the contract entered into in June, 1860. Similar purchases, for the purpose of arming their militia, were at that day, and are at present, quite common to all the states, and there is no more justification or pretense for saying that the passage of the act of December, 1859, was part of a deep laid conspiracy to subvert the Union, than there would be for declaring hereafter, in the event of civil disturbances growing out of the presidential election just passed, that the state of Mississippi was fomenting and preparing for such an emergency, by the acts of her legislature, adopted two years ago, authorizing the purchase of Gatlin [sic] guns and other fire-arms.[71]

In other words, by 1876 the Mississippi Supreme Court was willing to lean over to the view that no presumption or even inference of illegality as being in aid of the rebellion would be indulged in to defeat a contract otherwise valid.

Similarly, the court refused to speculate on the mental state of a lender of money in 1861, in an action brought in 1871 to recover the amount loaned, where the defense was raised that the plaintiff knew the money was to be used for the purpose of equipping a company of cavalry to serve the Confederacy. In holding that the loan was valid and that the lender could recover, the court disposed of the defense in the following manner:

An analysis of the mind of the plaintiff, however, in the determination of the rights of these parties, would seem to be, upon principle, inadmissible. We conceive it to be the contract, not the intention or mental purpose, or expectation of either or all of these parties, which ought to control this question. . . . Upon the face of the obligation sued on it is

[71] *Ibid.*, 739.

wholly disconnected from all illegality, and it is quite as probable he was governed in the arrangement as much by his avarice or his devotion to his family as by his desire to serve the confederacy.[72]

To the freed Mississippi slave, reconstruction had a meaning all of its own. The legal problems of emancipation became, in fact, a distinct branch of reconstruction jurisprudence, forming a brilliant contrast to the antebellum body of thought on this subject and to the rest of the reconstruction cases already considered. If the pre-war cases seem so remote, even by 1866, as to be unreal, the main body of reconstruction jurisprudence has a certain stuffy, sophistical quality about it. Not so in the area of emancipation where, after all, the most direct impact of the rebellion was felt. Without exception, the opinions of the Mississippi appellate court which touched upon it reflect an awe surrounding the incredible truth of emancipation, as it penetrated the judicial mind in a variety of tangible ways.

One of the first cases came up in the April, 1866, term. In *Malone* v. *Mooring*,[73] the court considered the disposition of a bequest of "negroes to the amount of $3,350" in a will admitted to probate in 1857. The argument was made by certain of the legatees that this was a general legacy payable out of the general fund of the estate. After holding the bequest to be a specific one, which of course failed upon the destruction of the property, the court reminded the disappointed beneficiaries that those "legatees who received their shares before the general emancipation took effect, have suffered equally with those whose shares were not yet reduced to possession; and we do not see how these petitioners can stand on any better footing than their sisters, in regard to the claim for recompense or satisfaction out of the general estate, for the specific property which they have lost."

A problem which had caused the high court to suffer from

---

[72] Walker v. Jeffries, 45 Miss. 160, 166–67 (1871).   [73] 40 Miss. 247, 256 (1866).

something resembling xenophobia in the two decades before the war—the right of Negroes emancipated out of state to take property by will in Mississippi—recurred in *Berry* v. *Alsop*.[74] Once more the court carefully reviewed the list of precedents on the "liberal" side of this question, studiously avoiding the two "hard" cases of *Mitchell* v. *Wells* and *Heirn* v. *Bridault*, which unquestionably represented the official policy of the state on the brink of the Civil War.[75] Only at the close of a long opinion which upheld the right of freed Negroes to inherit by will, did the court in *Berry* so much as concede their existence in the Mississippi Reports, and thereby expressly repudiated in one terse paragraph the "reasoning" and the "judgment" of those cases.[76]

In a similar vein and treating a related problem, *Cowan* v. *Stamps* [77] passed on the validity of a will executed by a Mississippi testator who died in 1864 exactly 8 miles from federal lines and 20 from Confederate lines in a section of the country between the armies of the two belligerents. The will directed the executor to send all his slaves to Africa "to become free" out of the proceeds of the property of the estate. Conceding that the policy which was to prevail was that prevailing at the time of death, what was that policy in 1864?

The court paused momentarily at the threshold of its decision to comment on the erratic course of past public policy on emancipation: "Our attention is naturally first drawn to the matter of public policy, upon which we observe great if not marvelous changes, following each other in rapid succession during the last few years, with reference to emancipation." Brushing by the *Heirn* and *Mitchell* cases, the court next remarked: "Language certainly could not well be stronger, and the public policy of Mississippi from 1857 may be considered as indicated in the em-

---

[74] 45 Miss. 1 (1871).
[75] 37 Miss. 235 (1859); 37 Miss. 209 (1859). The Mitchell and Heirn cases denied free Negroes emancipated in other states to take property by will in Mississippi.
[76] 45 Miss. at 10.   [77] 46 Miss. 435 (1872).

phatic terms of the statute quoted, more strikingly enunciated in Heirn v. Bridault, and in Mitchell v. Wells." And it reviewed Mississippi's judicial and legislative policy on emancipation with the observation that there had been indeed "extraordinary vibrations of public policy on a single subject, in a few years." [78]

Then it bore into the analysis. First, the court described with precision the location of the testator's home relative to the opposing armies. It commented on the scouting activities of both sides. Then the court said:

This locality [testator's residence], while not wholly within the federal lines, was accessible thereto, and remained subject to the general control and influence of the federal authorities. The military power of the Confederacy gradually receded from that section and never returned. Confederate civil officers, it is true, as in other counties all over the state, continued to discharge their functions until others were appointed, but it may be said that long before the death of the testator, freedom had come permanently to his slaves. They remained upon the place, and remain there still, but they were as free to go as to stay. Slavery was no longer enforced as to them. They were substantially subject to the power and influences of the federal authorities. The laws of slavery were to them at an end. We infer that they purposely clung to the premises, with the view of succeeding to the title and ownership under the will. If, as to the appellants, the policy of freedom was not in April, 1864, in full operation, certainly the laws and conditions of slavery had long before then become inoperative and were never after in force. [79]

Interestingly, the "policy of freedom" which the court sought to pinpoint in time followed the actual military campaigns of the war and the effective occupation by the Union army. Since the Emancipation Proclamation of 1863 was, according to the Mississippi court, not effectual "beyond emancipation in fact," [80] and since "the rights of the respective parties were fixed at the mo-

[78] *Ibid.*, 439–41.   [79] *Ibid.*, 444.
[80] *Ibid.*; see also McMath v. Johnson, 41 Miss. 439 (1867); and Vicksburg & Meridian R.R. v. Green, 42 Miss. 436 (1869).

ment of the death of the testator, by the law in force at that time," it became necessary for the court to recreate, with some accuracy, the historical scene surrounding the death of the testator. The court held that the "policy of freedom embraced and prevailed over the parties and interests in this controversy." [81]

Contracts for the sale of slaves entered into before or during the war provided a rich source of litigation after 1865. The conventional format of the cases was a suit on a promissory note given for the consideration of slaves, together with a warranty by the seller that they were "slaves for life." At issue was the merit of the defense that the warranty had been "broken" by the subsequent emancipation of the slaves. *Bradford* v. *Jenkins* [82] construed such a warranty as undertaking only "to guarantee the status of the slaves as slaves for life at the time of the sale, and the covenant is fulfilled if, at the time of the sale, the slaves were, by the then existing laws of the State, in a condition which rendered them liable to servitude for the period of their lives." The loss fell on the buyer; and if such a result seemed to him unjust, the court recited the rule that "every owner of property holds the same subject to such action as the sovereign power of the State may, in the exercise of its ultimate sovereignty, adopt in relation to it." [83]

Considering the effect of the clause in the Mississippi constitution of 1865, abrogating slavery in Mississippi, the court said: "Only such contracts come within the condemnation of this law, or its policy, as are entered into after its adoption, and which assumes the continued existence of the institution in the State. We cannot give to either a retrospective operation, so as to destroy rights vested by lawful contracts at a time when slavery was a cherished relation among us." [84]

[81] 46 Miss. at 443–44.   [82] 41 Miss. 328 (1867).   [83] *Ibid.*, 335.
[84] *Ibid.*, 337.

CONCLUSIONS

1. A striking pattern began early to emerge from the Mississippi reconstruction cases. Roughly two conflicting schools of thought came into being bearing (a) on the nature of the state's internal character during the Confederacy and reconstruction and (b) on its relation to the federal government during the same periods. The school of thought represented by *Hill* v. *Boyland* held that a viable de facto government existed in Mississippi during secession, with the authority to enact legislation which survived the Confederacy, and that the state's relations with the federal government remained unaltered by the Civil War.

2. This thesis was matched by the antithesis of *Thomas* v. *Taylor*, i.e., that the government of Mississippi from 1861 to 1865 was a revolutionary band and its acts mere nullities in contemplation of law. As for the state's relation to the federal government, it was virtually a conquered province at the mercy of federal military power.

3. From *Texas* v. *White* came the synthesis which distinguished between "state" and "government," holding that acts in aid of the rebellion were void, but those pertaining to purely private matters valid.

4. While pure theory occupied the Mississippi High Court in the early reconstruction cases, which often bogged down in paradoxes or straddled impossible dilemmas, practical reason and public policy prevailed as the basis of decision in the later phase of reconstruction. Gradually, as reconstruction theory became refined and articulated by the accumulation of precedents and as the effect of *Texas* v. *White* was felt, the crude, initial line of division which separated the two schools faded away, and it was eventually possible to cite cases representing either school of thought in support of a decision which was already predictable.

5. In its approach to problems growing out of emancipation, the high court embraced a policy of freedom which liberally

applied the emancipation-in-fact doctrine to the benefit of the free Negro in matters of testamentary bequests.

6. Groping through a period without precedent in the jurisprudence of the state or nation, the Mississippi High Court watched the United States Supreme Court more closely and manifested a willingness to follow its policy and its rules more genuinely than ever before in its history.

Recapitulation and Reflections

Given the major premise that the high court was a legal-political institution functioning in a philosophically deviant state, and given the minor premise that the immediate objective of the court was to find an acceptable legal rationalization for the concrete decision, what manner of court was this changing body of three men, all of whom sprang from or were nourished by the intellectual climate of antebellum Mississippi? Cryptically speaking, it was the best and the worst of all possible courts—enlightened and myopic, rational and irrational, compassionate and cruel, just and unjust, intellectually honest and dishonest. The Mississippi High Court simply embodied the noblest and the basest of the qualities of the society in which it flourished.

To measure the performance of the court by its treatment of the issue of race may seem arbitrary, in view of the several criteria of evaluation one might employ. Yet, it is a plausible criterion for several reasons. First, the frequency of the court's contacts with race is striking. Four chapters in this study have touched upon that point either squarely or obliquely. Second, race was the most critical issue which the high court had to face, and it exposed the court's most sensitive nerve. Third, the court was at its most brilliant and most barbaric in its response to race, a combination which deserves further comment. Fourth, the critical remarks which follow will connect with a final question to be raised in the recapitulation.

The chapters on criminal justice and manumission present the unusual combination of brilliance and barbarism referred to above. That manumission showed the court at its worst is too obvious to belabor. Its legal rationalizations were thin veils to cover fixed prejudices, and the emotional content of the opinions deprives them of any intellectual respect. Why was the same court so different in its role of protector of the Negro slave from the potential severity of the criminal law? Parenthetically, one remarkable revelation from the study is that throughout the period under review (1817–75) the harshness toward and contempt for the black man which, incidentally, became manifest in the opinions of the court *after* reconstruction, are noticeably absent from the opinions of the antebellum high court. Rather, one is impressed again and again by the court's sympathetic, almost indulgent, treatment of the black slave—except, of course, where the issue at stake concerned the law of resistance and rebellion.

A credible explanation for the contrasting positions of the court lies at the heart of the two chapters. Manumission threatened the very foundation and continuing existence of the society which had slavery as its base. The court could not, according to its scale of values, afford the luxury of liberality, for to do so would be to abandon its deepest convictions and enter the camp of the abolitionist enemy. Compromise was out of the question because there could be no middle ground. Either the black man was a slave or he was not, and all attempts to emancipate him undermined the institution of slavery.

In the area of criminal law, however, not only was there no corresponding threat to the structure of society, but the very real interest of the high court in preserving the quality of criminal justice in Mississippi and in preventing the law itself from degenerating into barbarism outweighed any repressive tendencies which the court might otherwise have held toward the Negro slave. So long as he *was* a slave, squarely, securely, and forever more, surely it was not too much to ask of county prosecutors and sheriffs that a confession not be beaten or tortured out of him. This was, essentially, the thinking of the high court.

The pair of chapters on the contract clause and the clause in the constitution of 1832 prohibiting the introduction of slaves as merchandise offers an interesting combination. Both brought the Mississippi High Court into direct confrontation with the Supreme Court of the United States, and both contained highly technical legal issues imbedded in the larger public policy at stake. There the similarity ends. In one, the high court won its bout with the nation's highest court, in that it spoke the last word on the contract clause; but ultimately it suffered a net loss of intellectual integrity by the use of legal legerdemain and by its distortion of one of its own earlier opinions to emasculate the contract clause. In the chapter on the prohibitory clause, the high court lost its bout with the Supreme Court, but gained respect for its dogged efforts to prevent a purely state policy from subversion by its federal adversary.

Considering that the problems discussed in the study were all public issues of critical importance at the time, the Mississippi High Court suffered remarkably little from internal rifts across the years. Compare in this regard the exertions of the court in 1859 to repair the deep cleft in the law of manumission and to speak as one man on this subject, with the bewildering oscillation on the bench between the opposing theories of reconstruction. But then, reconstruction stands out as the anomalous chapter of the study. The old pattern was broken but a new one had not yet emerged. For all its lack of outer direction and for all its inner confusion on reconstruction doctrine, the high court in 1866 could still hold the Civil Rights Act of 1866 unconstitutional. Indeed, never was the high court abject or repentant.

The final question which arrests the imagination is an engaging one. Might the high court of antebellum Mississippi have chosen other directions and traveled other roads in its response to the issues of its day? Focusing momentarily on the problem of the contract clause which lay at the core of Chapter 2, the answer is a decided *no*. So obdurate, so confident was the court of its power over its own banks (as illusory as this power actually was), that any softening of tone or a revision of doctrine seems remote. The same comment might apply equally well to the chapter on the constitutional clause prohibiting the introduction of slaves as merchandise, except that in this instance the power to nullify contracts made in violation of the clause was real, not illusory, and it is knowledge of this fact which kindles our sympathy. We would not want the court to have behaved any differently in Chapter 3. Turning to Chapter 5 and the unfolding of criminal justice in antebellum Mississippi, one could scarcely hope for a more humane, yet scholarly, body of law.

Thus, the question posed boils down to the issue of race again, and, in particular, to the opinions of the high court on manumission. Could the court have charted a nobler course in its approach to emancipation? As a point of departure it must be emphasized that the high court had a fairly explicit statutory guide to follow in this field. It was not free to "make" the law of manumission by judicial decision alone, but had perforce to implement the legislative policy embodied in the act of 1842. Even so, there was still room for a degree of judicial disobedience to and interpretation of the statute. Proof of this statement lies in the two conflicting lines of decision on the issue which had first taken root, and then developed deliberately and concurrently up until the year 1859. One represented the "soft," the other the "hard" wing of the court. As late as 1858—the year of the high-water "soft" decision of *Shaw* v. *Brown*—it was still conceivable that this "soft" wing might prevail and the court avoid its flight from reason which took place the following year with *Mitchell* v. *Wells*. The question now narrows into a search for some fact or event which transpired between the April term, 1858, when *Shaw* was decided, and the April term, 1859, when *Mitchell* came down, which may have induced the court to swing over to the *Mitchell* doctrine.

On the bench at the moment of the *Shaw* decision sat the Chief Justice Cotesworth Smith, together with Justices Ephraim Fisher and Alexander Handy. Justice Handy delivered the moderate opinion of the court in *Shaw;* Justice Fisher voted with Handy, and the chief justice did not sit in this case for some unknown reason. Judge Fisher, the concurring justice, resigned in November, 1858, his successor, William Harris, taking office in November of that year. Significantly, Justice Harris delivered the incredibly "hard" opinion of the court in *Mitchell*. The chief justice now voted with Harris but wrote no opinion. Justice Handy dissented in a twenty-three-page opinion. In a capsule, one justice—Alexander Handy—was decidedly liberal on the manumission issue; one justice—William Harris—was intensely tough; and the chief justice—Cotesworth Smith—uncommitted. At the critical moment Smith, the holder of the balance of power, threw his lot in with Harris, as the court swiftly felled the entire line of "soft" cases in bulldozer fashion, and reached its nadir of judicial rationalization.

One ultimate conclusion might be that Justice Handy emerges as the lonely, courageous dissenter in this most sensitive of issues confronting the antebellum court. Only up to a point. A man of courage and compassion, yes; but a prophet, no. While he deprecated the court's opinion in *Mitchell* for its severity and for carrying the policy of the act of 1842 beyond its legislative intent, his position correctly and narrowly drawn was that Negroes freed by sister states should be able to take property by will in Mississippi. On the fundamental values and larger issues he was entirely "sound"—that is, he believed in the institution of slavery, the doctrine of state sovereignty, and the compact theory of government.

Handy's degree of deviation is the most that one could hope to find in the opinions of the antebellum high court. It is highly unlikely that the Mississippi body politic of that era could have produced an apostate of real strength and grandeur. It is even more improbable that that society would have elevated him to the high court if it had, by some historical accident, produced him. And it is inconceivable that this apostate would have been allowed to flourish for long, if he had indeed found his way to the high court.

In the end, we might wonder whether the high court is more to be admired for the intensity of its faith and for its intrepidity in legal battle, to be pitied for the blindness imposed upon it by the society which created it, or reviled for its arrogance and self-righteousness in defending the values of that society.

SELECTIVE BIBLIOGRAPHY

BOOKS

Bettersworth, John K. *Mississippi: A History.* Austin, Tex.: Steck Company, 1959.

Biographical and Historical Memoirs of Mississippi. Vol. I. Chicago: Goodspeed Publishing Company, 1891.

Black's Law Dictionary. 4th ed. St. Paul, Minn.: West Publishing Co., 1951.

Burgess, John W. *Reconstruction and the Constitution.* New York: Charles Scribner's Sons, 1907.

Carter, Clarence E., comp. and ed. *The Territorial Papers of the United States.* Vol. V: *The Territory of Mississippi, 1798–1817.* Washington, D.C.: United States Government Printing Office, 1937.

Cash, Wilbur J. *The Mind of the South.* New York: Alfred A. Knopf, 1941.

Claiborne, J. F. H. *Life and Correspondence of John A. Quitman.* 2 vols. New York: Harper and Bros., 1860.

————. *Mississippi, As a Province, Territory and State.* Jackson, Miss.: Power and Barksdale, 1880. Reprinted by Louisiana State University Press, 1964.

Cluskey, M. W., ed. *Speeches, Messages, and Other Writings of Albert G. Brown.* 2d ed. Philadelphia: Jas. B. Smith and Company, 1859.

Crallé, Richard K., ed. *Works of Calhoun.* Vol. I, *Disquisition on Government.* Charleston, S.C.: Steam Power-Press of Walker and James, 1851. Vols. II–IV, *Speeches.* Vols. V–VI, *Reports and Public Letters.* New York: D. Appleton and Company, 1853–55.

163

Craven, Avery O. *The Growth of Southern Nationalism 1848–1861.* A History of the South Series, Vol. VI. Baton Rouge, La.: Louisiana State University Press and the Littlefield Fund for Southern History of the University of Texas, 1953.

Davis, Jefferson. *The Rise and Fall of the Confederate Government.* 2 vols. New York: D. Appleton and Company, 1881.

Ethridge, George H. *Mississippi, A History.* Vol. I. Jackson, Miss.; Hopkinsville, Ky.; Shreveport, La.: Historical Record Association, n.d.

————. *Mississippi Constitutions.* Jackson, Miss.: Tucker Printing House, 1928.

Garner, James G. *Reconstruction in Mississippi.* New York: Macmillan Company, 1901.

Harris, William C. *Presidential Reconstruction in Mississippi.* Baton Rouge, La.: Louisiana State University Press, 1967.

Hearon, Cleo. *Mississippi and the Compromise of 1850.* Publications of the Mississippi Historical Society, Vol. XIV. University, Miss.: Printed for the Society, 1914.

Kirwan, Albert D. *Revolt of the Rednecks, Mississippi Politics 1876–1925.* Lexington, Ky.: University of Kentucky Press, 1951.

Lynch, James D. *The Bench and Bar of Mississippi.* New York: E. J. Hale and Son, 1881.

McKitrick, Eric L. *Andrew Johnson and Reconstruction.* Chicago: University of Chicago Press, 1960.

Rainwater, Percy L. *Mississippi: Storm Center of Secession 1856–1861.* Baton Rouge, La.: Otto Claitor, 1938.

Rowland, Dunbar. *Courts, Judges and Lawyers of Mississippi, 1798–1935.* Jackson, Miss.: Hederman Bros. Press, 1935.

————, ed. *Jefferson Davis, Constitutionalist: His Letters, Papers and Speeches.* 10 vols. Jackson, Miss.: Printed for the Mississippi Department of Archives and History by the Press of J. J. Little and Ives Company, New York, 1923.

————, ed. and comp. *The Mississippi Territorial Archives, 1798–1803.* Nashville, Tenn.: Press of Brandon Printing Company, 1905.

Stampp, Kenneth. *The Era of Reconstruction, 1865–1877.* New York: Alfred A. Knopf, 1965.

Sydnor, Charles S. *Slavery in Mississippi.* New York: D. Appleton-Century Company, 1933.

Wharton, Vernon L. *The Negro in Mississippi 1865–1890.* The James Sprunt Studies in History and Political Science, Vol. XXVIII. Chapel Hill, N.C.: University of North Carolina Press, 1947.

ARTICLES

Drake, Winbourne M. "The Mississippi Reconstruction Convention of 1865." *Journal of Mississippi History*, XXI (October, 1959), 225–56.

Woods, Thomas H. "A Sketch of the Mississippi Secession Convention of 1861,—Its Membership and Work." *Publications of the Mississippi Historical Society*, VI (1902), 91–104.

NEWSPAPERS

New York Times, October 26, 1866.

LEGAL LITERATURE

Code of Mississippi (Hutchinson). *Being An Analytical Compilation of the Public and General Statutes of the Territory and State from 1798 to 1848.* Jackson, Miss.: Price and Fall, State Printers, 1848.

Digest of the Statutes of the Mississippi Territory (Toulmin). N.p., 1807.

Journal of the Convention of the State of Mississippi, 1851. Jackson, Miss.: Thomas Palmer, Printer, 1851.

Journal of the Proceedings and Debates in the Constitutional Convention, August 1865. Jackson, Miss.: E. M. Yerger, State Printer, 1865.

Journal of the Proceedings in the Constitutional Convention, 1868. Jackson, Miss.: E. Stafford, Printer, 1871.

Journal of the State Convention and Ordinances and Resolutions Adopted in January, 1861. Jackson, Miss.: E. Barksdale, State Printer, 1861.

Laws of Mississippi. 1822, 1830, 1833, 1842, 1844, 1846, 1860, 1865 (Called Session), and 1873.

Mississippi. Constitution. 1817, 1832, and 1869.

Revised Code of Mississippi (Sharkey, Ellett and Harris). Published by Authority of the Legislature. Jackson, Miss.: E. Barksdale, State Printer, 1857.

Revised Code of the Laws of Mississippi (Poindexter). Natchez, Miss.: Printed by Francis Baker, 1824.

Sargent's Code (1799–1800). Prepared by the Historical Records Survey Division of Professional and Service Projects, Works Progress Administration. Jackson, Miss.: Historical Records Survey, 1939.

Statutes of the Mississippi Territory (Turner). Digested by the Authority of the General Assembly. Natchez, Miss.: Printed by Peter Isler, 1816.

Statutes of the State of Mississippi (Howard and Hutchinson). By Authority. New Orleans, La.: E. Johns and Company, 1840.

U.S. Constitution.

U.S. Statutes at Large. Vols. I, II, V, IX, XII, XIV, and XV.

CASES CITED

Ableman v. Booth, 62 U.S. (21 How.) 506 (1858).

Abram v. State, 25 Miss. 589 (1853).

Adams v. Rowan, 16 Miss. (8 S. & M.) 624 (1847).

Alcorn v. Hamer, 38 Miss. 562 (1860).

Mrs. Alexander's Cotton, 69 U.S. (2 Wall.) 404 (1864).

Alfred v. State, 37 Miss. 296 (1859).

The Amy Warwick, 1 F. Cas. 808 (No. 342) (D.C.D. Mass.) 1862.

Bailey v. Fitz-gerald, 56 Miss. 578 (1879).

Baldwin v. Payne, 47 U.S. (6 How.) 332 (1848).

Bank of Augusta v. Earle, 38 U.S. (13 Pet.) 519 (1839).

Barksdale v. Elam, 30 Miss. 694 (1856).

Beall v. State, 39 Miss. 715 (1861).

Beatty v. Smith, 10 Miss. (2 S. & M.) 567 (1844).

Beauchamp v. Comfort, 42 Miss. 94 (1868).

Belote v. State, 36 Miss. 96 (1858).

Benoit v. Bell, 15 Miss. (7 S. & M.) 32 (1846).

Berry v. Alsop, 45 Miss. 1 (1871).

Blanchard's Administrators v. Buckholt's Administrators, 1 Miss.
    (Walk.) 64 (1818).

Boles v. State, 21 Miss. (13 S. & M.) 398 (1850).

Bradford v. Jenkins, 41 Miss. 328 (1867).

Brian v. Davidson, 25 Miss. 213 (1852).

Brien v. Williamson, 8 Miss. (7 How.) 14 (1843).

Brown v. Beatty, 34 Miss. 227 (1857).

Brown v. State, 32 Miss. 433 (1856).

Buchanan v. Smith, 43 Miss. 90 (1870).

Buck v. Vasser, 47 Miss. 551 (1873).

Butler v. Hicks, 19 Miss. (11 S. & M.) 78 (1848).

Byrd v. State, 2 Miss. (1 How.) 163 (1834).

Calder v. Bull, 3 U.S. (3 Dall.) 386 (1798).

Carpenter v. State, 5 Miss. (4 How.) 163 (1839).

Carter v. Burris, 18 Miss. (10 S. & M.) 527 (1848).

Cassell v. Backrack, 42 Miss. 56 (1868).

Cheairs v. Smith, 37 Miss. 646 (1859).

Chew v. Calvert, 1 Miss. (Walk.) 54 (1818).

Chisholm v. Georgia, 2 U.S. (2 Dall.) 419 (1793).

Collins v. McCargo, 14 Miss. (16 S. & M.) 128 (1846).

Commercial Bank v. Chambers, 16 Miss. (8 S. & M.) 2 (1847).

Commercial Bank v. State, 14 Miss. (6 S. & M.) 599 (1846).
Commercial Bank v. State, 20 Miss. (4 S. & M.) 439 (1845).
Conger v. Robinson, 12 Miss. (4 S. & M.) 210 (1845).
Coon v. State, 21 Miss. (13 S. & M.) 246 (1849).
Cotton v. State, 31 Miss. 504 (1856).
Cowan v. Stamps, 46 Miss. 435 (1872).
Craig v. Missouri, 29 U.S. (4 Pet.) 410 (1830).
Curll v. Compton, 22 Miss. (14 S. & M.) 56 (1850).
Dartmouth College Case, 17 U.S. (4 Wheat.) 518 (1819).
Deans v. McLendon, 30 Miss. 343 (1855).
Delmas v. Insurance Co., 81 U.S. (14 Wall.) 661 (1871).
Dennistoun and Co. v. Potts, 26 Miss. 2 (1853).
Donovan v. Mayor and Council of Vicksburg, 29 Miss. 247 (1855).
Dorsey v. Maury, 18 Miss. (10 S. & M.) 298 (1848).
Doughty v. Owen, 24 Miss. 404 (1852).
Dowell v. Boyd, 11 Miss. (3 S. & M.) 592 (1844).
Dowling v. State, 13 Miss. (5 S. & M.) 664 (1846).
Dyson v. State, 26 Miss. 362 (1853).
Ex parte Dyson, 25 Miss. 356 (1852).
Edwards v. Williams, 3 Miss. (2 How.) 846 (1838).
Elmendorf v. Taylor, 23 U.S. (10 Wheat.) 152 (1825).
Fairly Administrators v. Fairly, 38 Miss. 280 (1859).
Files v. McWilliams, 49 Miss. 578 (1873).
Ford v. Surget, 46 Miss. 130 (1871).
Ford v. Surget, 97 U.S. 594 (1878).
Foster v. Alston, 7 Miss. (6 How.) 406 (1842).
Fox v. Ohio, 46 U.S. (5 How.) 410 (1847).
Frank v. State, 39 Miss. 705 (1861).
Frazer v. Robinson, 42 Miss. 121 (1868).
Garnett v. Cowles, 39 Miss. 60 (1860).
George v. State, 37 Miss. 316 (1859).
Gibbons v. Ogden, 22 U.S. (9 Wheat.) 1 (1824).
Glidewell v. Hite, 6 Miss. (5 How.) 110 (1840).
Grand Gulf R.R. v. State, 18 Miss. (10 S. & M.) 428 (1848).
The Grapeshot, 76 U.S. (9 Wall.) 129 (1869).
Green v. Robinson, 6 Miss. (5 How.) 80 (1840).
Green v. Sizer, 40 Miss. 530 (1866).
Green v. Weller, 32 Miss. 650 (1856).
Griffin v. Mixon, 38 Miss. 424 (1860).
Griffing v. Hopkins, 1 Miss. (Walk.) 49 (1818).
Groves v. Slaughter, 40 U.S. (15 Pet.) 449 (1841).
Hare v. State, 5 Miss. (4 How.) 187 (1839).

Harlan v. State, 41 Miss. 566 (1867).

Harmon v. Short, 16 Miss. (8 S. & M.) 433 (1847).

Harris v. Runnels, 53 U.S. (12 How.) 79 (1851).

Harry v. Decker, 1 Miss. (Walk.) 36 (1818).

Heirn v. Bridault, 37 Miss. 209 (1859).

Henderson v. Poindexter's Lessee, 25 U.S. (12 Wheat.) 530 (1827).

Hill v. Boyland, 40 Miss. 618 (1866).

Hinds v. Brazealle, 3 Miss. (2 How.) 837 (1838).

Hinds v. Terry, 1 Miss. (Walk.) 80 (1820).

Holt v. Barton, 42 Miss. 711 (1869).

Houston v. Burney, 10 Miss. (2 S. & M.) 583 (1844).

Isham v. State, 7 Miss. (6 How.) 35 (1841).

Isom v. Mississippi Central R.R., 36 Miss. 300 (1858).

James v. Elder, 23 Miss. 134 (1851).

James v. Herring, 20 Miss. (12 S. & M.) 336 (1849).

Jennings v. Gibson, 1 Miss. (Walk.) 234 (1826).

Jones v. Van Zandt, 46 U.S. (5 How.) 215 (1847).

Jordan v. State, 32 Miss. 382 (1856).

Josephine v. State, 39 Miss. 613 (1860).

Judge of Probate v. Alexander, 31 Miss. 297 (1856).

Kelly v. State, 11 Miss. (3 S. & M.) 518 (1844).

Kinley v. Fitzpatrick, 5 Miss. (4 How.) 59 (1839).

Lacoste v. Pipkin, 21 Miss. (13 S. & M.) 589 (1850).

Lamar v. Williams, 39 Miss. 342 (1860).

Leachman v. Musgrove, 45 Miss. 511 (1871).

Leathers v. State, 26 Miss. 73 (1853).

Leech v. Cooley, 14 Miss. (6 S. & M.) 93 (1846).

Legal Tender Cases, 79 U.S. (12 Wall.) 457 (1870).

Leiper v. Hoffman, 26 Miss. 615 (1853).

Lewis v. State, 17 Miss. (9 S. & M.) 115 (1847).

Lewis's Administrators v. Farrish, 2 Miss. (1 How.) 547 (1837).

Long v. Hickingbottom, 28 Miss. 772 (1855).

Luckey v. Dykes, 10 Miss. (2 S. & M.) 60 (1843).

Lusk v. Lewis, 32 Miss. 297 (1856).

McCulloch v. Maryland, 17 U.S. (4 Wheat.) 316 (1819).

McIntyre v. Ingraham, 35 Miss. 25 (1858).

McMath v. Johnson, 41 Miss. 439 (1867).

Mahorner v. Hooe, 17 Miss. (9 S. & M.) 247 (1848).

Malone v. Mooring, 40 Miss. 247 (1866).

Marbury v. Madison, 5 U.S. (1 Cranch) 137 (1803).

Martin v. Hunter's Lessee, 14 U.S. (1 Wheat.) 304 (1816).

Mask v. State, 32 Miss. 405 (1856).

Miller v. United States, 78 U.S. (11 Wall.) 268 (1870).
Minor v. State, 36 Miss. 630 (1859).
Mississippi Central R.R. v. State, 46 Miss. 157 (1871).
Mitchell v. Wells, 37 Miss. 235 (1859).
Montgomery v. Galbraith, 19 Miss. (11 S. & M.) 555 (1848).
Moore v. Illinois, 55 U.S. (14 How.) 13 (1852).
Moore v. State, 36 Miss. 137 (1858).
Mount v. Harris, 9 Miss. (1 S. & M.) 185 (1843).
Murphy v. Clark, 9 Miss. (1 S. & M.) 221 (1843).
Murphy v. State, 24 Miss. 590 (1852).
Murrell v. Jones, 40 Miss. 565 (1866).
Nevitt v. Bank of Port Gibson, 14 Miss. (6 S. & M.) 513 (1846).
Newcomb v. State, 37 Miss. 383 (1859).
Newell v. Newell, 17 Miss. (9 S. & M.) 56 (1847).
Newman v. Montgomery, 6 Miss. (5 How.) 742 (1841).
Nixon v. State, 10 Miss. (2 S. & M.) 497 (1844).
Noel v. Wheatley, 30 Miss. 181 (1855).
Oliver v. State, 39 Miss. 526 (1860).
Payne v. Baldwin, 11 Miss. (3 S. & M.) 661 (1844).
Peter v. State, 12 Miss. (4 S. & M.) 31 (1844).
Planters Bank v. Sharp, 12 Miss. (4 S. & M.) 3 (1844).
Planters' Bank v. Sharp, 47 U.S. (6 How.) 301 (1848).
Prigg v. Pennsylvania, 41 U.S. (16 Pet.) 539 (1842).
The Prize Cases, 67 U.S. (2 Black) 635 (1862).
Randal v. State, 12 Miss. (4 S. & M.) 349 (1845).
Read v. Manning, 30 Miss. 308 (1855).
Riggs v. State, 26 Miss. 51 (1853).
Ross v. Vertner, 6 Miss. (5 How.) 305 (1840).
Runnels v. State, 1 Miss. (Walk.) 146 (1823).
Saffarans v. Terry, 20 Miss. (12 S. & M.) 690 (1849).
Sam v. Fore, 20 Miss. (12 S. & M.) 413 (1849).
Sam v. State, 31 Miss. 480 (1856).
Sam v. State, 33 Miss. 347 (1857).
Sarah v. State, 28 Miss. 267 (1854).
Scott v. Bilgerry, 40 Miss. 119 (1866).
Scott v. Sandford, 60 U.S. (19 How.) 393 (1858).
Serpentine v. State, 2 Miss. (1 How.) 256 (1835).
Shattuck v. Daniel, 52 Miss. 834 (1876).
Shattuck v. Young, 10 Miss. (2 S. & M.) 30 (1844).
Shaw v. Brown, 35 Miss. 246 (1858).
Shewalter v. Ford, 34 Miss. 417 (1857).
Shotwell v. Ellis and Co., 42 Miss. 439 (1869).

Simon v. State, 37 Miss. 288 (1859).
Smith's Administrator v. Smith, 2 Miss. (1 How.) 102 (1834).
Sprott v. United States, 87 U.S. (20 Wall.) 459 (1874).
State v. Anderson, 11 Miss. (3 S. & M.) 751 (1844).
State v. Johnson, 25 Miss. 625 (1853).
State v. Jones, 1 Miss. (Walk.) 83 (1821).
State v. McGinty, 41 Miss. 435 (1867).
State v. McGraw, 1 Miss. (Walk.) 208 (1825).
State v. Moor, 1 Miss. (Walk.) 134 (1823).
State v. Smedes, 26 Miss. 47 (1853).
Strader v. Graham, 51 U.S. (10 How.) 82 (1850).
Stringfellow v. State, 26 Miss. 157 (1853).
Taylor v. Thomas, 89 U.S. (22 Wall.) 479 (1874).
Texas v. White, 74 U.S. (7 Wall.) 700 (1868).
Thomas v. Phillips, 12 Miss. (14 S. & M.) 358 (1845).
Thomas v. Taylor, 42 Miss. 651 (1869).
Thompson v. Grand Gulf R.R., 4 Miss. (3 How.) 240 (1839).
Thornton v. Demoss, 13 Miss. (5 S. & M.) 609 (1846).
Trotter v. McCall, 26 Miss. 410 (1853).
Trotter v. Trotter, 40 Miss. 704 (1866).
Turnbull v. Middleton, 1 Miss. (Walk.) 413 (1831).
United States v. Klein, 80 U.S. (13 Wall.) 128 (1871).
Van Buren v. State, 24 Miss. 512 (1852).
The Venice, 69 U.S. (2 Wall.) 258 (1864).
Vicksburg and Meridian R.R. v. Green, 42 Miss. 536 (1869).
Wade v. American Colonization Society, 15 Miss. (7 S. & M.) 663
    (1846).
Walker v. Jeffries, 45 Miss. 160 (1871).
Wash v. State, 22 Miss. (14 S. & M.) 120 (1850).
Wesley v. State, 37 Miss. 327 (1859).
Whitney v. State, 52 Miss. 732 (1876).
Whooten v. Miller, 15 Miss. (7 S. & M.) 380 (1846).
Wilkinson v. Leland, 27 U.S. (2 Pet.) 627 (1829).
Williams v. Cammack, 27 Miss. 209 (1854).
Williams v. State, 32 Miss. 389 (1856).
Withers v. Buckley, 61 U.S. (20 How.) 84 (1857).
Young v. Thompson, 11 Miss. (3 S. & M.) 742 (1844).

GENERAL INDEX

Alcorn, James, 21 n
American Colonization Society: role in
   manumission of slaves, 76, 81-82, 84

Baldwin, Henry, 59 n
Brown, Albert Gallatin, 20

Calhoun, John C., 3, 14, 18 n
Childs, [Justice], 51
Claiborne, J. F. H., 67 n
Clayton, Alexander, 114
Comity, 25, 28, 71, 73-74, 85, 87-89
Compact theory of government: as formula
   for secession, 22-29; as interpreted by
   Calhoun, 22; as interpreted by Davis, 23;
   as interpreted by Hobbes, 22; federal
   doctrine of, 25-28; used by High Court,
   23-25
Composition of court: mass resignation in
   1869, pp. 142-143; shift in 1858, pp.
   161-162
Compromise of 1850, p. 19
Confederacy: identity of state during,
   125-127, 129, 145; validity of legislation
   during, 126-147
"Confederacy": as used by High Court, 28
Confederate Congress, 18, 124
Constitution of 1817: art. 1, § 1, p. 5; art. 5,

§ 11, p. 5; Declaration of rights, 94; manumission, 71, 74; slaves, importation as
   merchandise, 49, 53
Constitution of 1832: amended in 1865,
   p. 126; concept of popular sovereignty, 17;
   criminal procedural rights, enumerated,
   94-95; Declaration of Rights, 94; manumission, 71, 74; mode of amending,
   construed, 6; slaves, importation as merchandise, 52-62
Constitution of 1869, pp. 127, 148 n
Contracts: act of 1840 construed under,
   39-40; confrontation with U.S. Supreme
   Court concerning, 38-47; constitutional
   prohibition of, 32; impairment of, 31-47;
   sale of illegally imported slaves, 52-56,
   62-66
Criminal law: bail in capital cases, 102;
   counsel in capital cases, 95; court's position toward accused, 94, 96, 116-117, 122,
   158-159; disqualification of jurors for bias,
   103; disqualification of jurors for holding
   scruples against death penalty, 104;
   identification of charge for accused construed by court, 100-101; irregularities in
   jury selection, 103; misconduct of juries,
   105; privilege against self-incrimination,
   101-102; procedural rights guaranteed in
   1832 constitution, 94-95; slaves as sub-

171

Criminal Law (*continued*)
jects of criminal law, 105-121; speedy trial
construed by court, 99-100. *See also*
Slaves

Davis, Jefferson, 4, 14, 18
Declaration of Rights: enumerated in Constitution of 1832, pp. 94-95
Defender of the faith: court's role in manumission, 69
Due process: construed in 1832 constitution, 7-8

Ellett, Henry T., 142
Emancipation. *See* Manumission
Eminent domain: constitutional provision
construed, 5-6

Fisher, Ephraim, 161
Free Negroes: in Mississippi, 77, 91, 92

Handy, Alexander, 25, 126, 142, 161-162
Harris, William, 89, 113, 142, 161
Hobbes, Thomas, 22

Jeffords, [Justice], 143
Johnson, Andrew, 124, 127
Judicial review, 9

Law-equity jurisdiction, 55-56
Locke, John, 22

McLean, John, 59 n
Manumission: affecting comity, 71-74, 85,
87-89; as early threat to state, 70; emotional content of High Court's opinions,
68, 77, 158; High Court's attitude toward
Mississippi slaveholders, 71, 77, 78-83,
85-87; High Court's attitude toward non-
slaveholding states, 70, 77, 83-84, 90-91;
High Court's role in, 70-93, 160-162; legal
structure of, 71-77; petitions for freedom,
70, 75; role of American Colonization
Society, 76, 81-82, 84; schism on court
over, 82-85, 91-93; as transitional stage,
75
Missouri Compromise, 8 n

Ord, Edward, 127

Peyton, [Justice], 143

Quitman, John A., 4, 14, 15 n, 19-20

Reconstruction, 123-155; constitutional
convention of 1865, pp. 126, 153; dilemma faced by state, 125-126, 129; "conquered province" theory, 124; "presidential" theory, 124; impact of on freed
slaves, 150-153; impact of *Texas* v. *White*
on court, 123, 124, 154; military government in Mississippi, 143; name of court
changed during, 143 n; reconstruction
acts, 134 n, 143; role of court during,
126-155; significance of *Texas* v. *White*,
143-145, 154; Supreme Court, decisional
law on, 124
Revised Code of 1857, pp. 46, 76
Rousseau, Jean J., 22

Secession: as constitutional right, 19-20,
140; as revolutionary, 19-20; date, 18;
declaration of causes, 20-21; ordinance of,
20-21; effect of ordinance during reconstruction, 128; ordinance repealed, 126
Shackleford, [Justice], 143
Sharkey, William L., 4, 35, 49, 51 n, 53, 56,
80, 113, 126
Slaveholders: attempts to emancipate by
will, 71; adherence to law, 82, 85-91;
circumvention of law, 79-82; distinguished from slavetraders, 52-53, 68;
limited by law, 75-76
Slavery: abolition of, 126; as institution, 53,
93, 153; growing population, 48 n, 53
Slaves: act of 1822 concerning convicts and
African-born, 62; as chattels, 49-52; confessions, coerced, 116-119, 122; constitution of 1832, pp. 52-67; crimes by, against
slaves, 110; crimes by, against whites,
110-111; duty of submission vs. rights of
resistance, 114-116; murder of, 106 n,
108-110; person-chattel dichotomy in
legal system, 105-107, 113; presumption
of, 49; as privileged communications,
121-122; prohibition against importing
convicts and African-born, 52; public policy against importation as merchandise,
52-54, 56, 58-61, 65-66; res of trusts, 50;
right of appeal, 112-113; right of creditors
to levy on, 50; source of rights to, 108;
special code of laws for, 106; specific
performance, 51; as subjects of criminal

CASES INDEX

Ableman v. *Booth*, 27, 72 n
Abram v. *State*, 103 n
Adams v. *Rowan*, 62 n
Alcorn v. *Hamer*, 6, 17, 23, 26
The Amy Warwick, 129

Baldwin v. *Payne*, 39, 40, 42
Bank of Augusta v. *Earle*, 73
Barksdale v. *Elam*, 49 n
Beall v. *State*, 102
Beatty v. *Smith*, 51 n
Beauchamp v. *Comfort*, 135 n
Belote v. *State*, 120
Benoit v. *Bell*, 70 n
Berry v. *Alsop*, 151
Boles v. *State*, 105 n
Brian v. *Davidson*, 51 n
Brien v. *Williamson*, 53-54, 58-61, 63
Brown v. *Beatty*, 5
Brown v. *State*, 119
Buchanan v. *Smith*, 146
Buck v. *Vassar*, 146
Butler v. *Hicks*, 51 n
Byrd v. *State*, 103

Calder v. *Bull*, 26
Carpenter v. *State*, 103 n
Cassell v. *Backrack*, 135, 141
Cheairs v. *Smith*, 83 n
Chisholm v. *Georgia*, 16, 25

Collins v. *McCargo*, 62 n
Commercial Bank v. *Chambers*, 38
Commercial Bank v. *State*, 36, 37
Conger v. *Robinson*, 50 n
Coon v. *State*, 50 n, 107 n
Cotton v. *State*, 103 n
Cowan v. *Stamps*, 151
Craig v. *Missouri*, 61
Curll v. *Compton*, 50 n

Dartmouth College Case, 31
Deans v. *McLendon*, 70
Dennistoun and Co. v. *Potts*, 10
Dorsey v. *Maury*, 24
Doughty v. *Owen*, 107
Dowell v. *Boyd*, 52 n
Dyson v. *State*, 96

Edwards v. *Williams*, 106 n
Elmendorf v. *Taylor*, 57
Ex parte Dyson, 102

Fairly Adm'rs v. *Fairly*, 50 n
Files v. *McWilliams*, 148 n
Ford v. *Surget*, 137
Fox v. *Ohio*, 97
Frazer v. *Robinson*, 135 n

Garnett v. *Cowles*, 83 n
George v. *State*, 110

F 1086	DATE DUE		

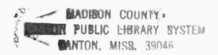